AMERICAN PATRIOTS

THE STORY OF BLACKS
IN THE MILITARY
FROM THE REVOLUTION
TO DESERT STORM

BY **GAIL BUCKLEY** ADAPTED FOR YOUNG PEOPLE BY **TONYA BOLDEN**

Crown Publishers New York

For Kevin
—G.B.

For Divivian Jerome-McGuire, who understands the importance
of knowing history. May all your strivings be blessed.
—T.B.

Adapted from *American Patriots: The Story of Blacks in the Military from the Revolution
to Desert Storm,* published by Random House in 2001.

CROWN and colophon are trademarks of Random House, Inc.

www.randomhouse.com/kids

Library of Congress Cataloging-in-Publication Data
Bolden, Tonya.
American patriots : the story of blacks in the military from the Revolution to Desert
Storm / by Gail Buckley ; adapted for young people by Tonya Bolden. — 1st ed.
p. cm.
Summary: Presents the story of the black experience in United States military history.
Includes bibliographical references and index.
ISBN 0-375-82243-7 (trade) — ISBN 0-375-92243-1 (lib. bdg.)
1. African American soldiers—Biography—Juvenile literature. 2. African American
soldiers—History—Juvenile literature. 3. United States—History, Military—Juvenile
literature. 4. United States—Armed Forces—African Americans—History—Juvenile
literature. 5. United States—Race relations—Juvenile literature. [1. African American
soldiers. 2. United States—History, Military. 3. Race relations.]
I. Buckley, Gail Lumet, 1937– American patriots. II. Title.
E185.63 .B65 2003
355'.008996'73—dc21
2002073713

Printed in the United States of America
First Edition
January 2003
10 9 8 7 6 5 4 3 2 1

CONTENTS

INTRODUCTION

I was a child during World War II, a time when patriotism was high in America—and I was patriotic to the core. I knew the hymns of all the armed services. Behind my home in Hollywood, California, I had my own "Victory" garden, in which I grew I remember not—except for radishes. At the time, with food being rationed, I felt I was doing my part for the war effort: the more food civilians grew and canned, the more factories would be freed up to produce things the military needed.

Members of my family were patriotic, too. My mother, Lena Horne, sang for GIs, as people began calling soldiers during World War II ("GI" stands for "Government Issue"). My great-uncle John Burke Horne was a sergeant in the Army, and he was engaged to my personal military role model, Lieutenant Harriet Pickens, who was in the Navy's WAVES (Women Accepted for Volunteer Emergency Service). However, I had no idea then that Uncle Burke was a sergeant in the *segregated* Army or that Harriet was one of the first *black* WAVES. As a child, I also had no idea that black GIs often sat behind German prisoners of war at United Service Organizations (USO) shows, and that my mother was banned from the USO for refusing to sing at such an event.

Years later, when I began to work on my book *The Hornes,* a family history, I discovered that Uncle John Burke's much older brother Errol had served in the military. He had made a career in the Army, then based in the faraway vastness of the West, home of the 9th and 10th Cavalries and 24th and 25th Infantries: the legendary Buffalo Soldier regiments.

Always a superb athlete, Errol was taught to ride horses and shoot by veterans of the Indian Wars, at Fort Huachuca, in the Arizona desert. Black soldiers regularly won top prizes in marksmanship and riding competitions, which were among the very few nonsegregated activities in the Army. By 1916, handsome twenty-six-year-old Sergeant Horne was at the top of his profession. That year, he was a member of an all-black force, commanded by Brigadier General John J. Pershing, that went in hot pursuit of Pancho Villa. This Mexican revolutionary-bandit had led a raid on Columbus, New Mexico. In the raid, seven soldiers had been killed: members of the 24th Infantry and Sergeant Errol Horne's regiment, the 10th Cavalry.

In those days, sergeant was the highest rank to which a black soldier could aspire, but Errol Horne was promoted to lieutenant during World War I. Sadly, within a year of his arrival in France, Lieutenant Horne was dead: a victim of the influenza epidemic that swept the ranks of the American Expeditionary Forces and much of the world in the winter of 1918. It is impossible to know how much of the war Errol actually saw: his records were among those destroyed in a fire in the U.S. Army archives in 1973. There's no doubt in my mind, however, that my great-uncle Errol was a hero.

What do heroes do? They fight dragons. And black Americans have been fighting the dragons of racism since the uprising that gave birth to this nation. One of their most powerful weapons has been service in the military. In joining the armed forces, and in going to war, black men and women believed they could both better their own lives and make their country true to its own best promise. *American Patriots* is a celebration of their fortitude, a tribute to their heroism.

—Gail Buckley

THE REVOLUTION

I served in the Revolution, in General Washington's army. . . . I have stood in battle, where balls, like hail, were flying all around me. The man standing next to me was shot by my side—his blood spouted upon my clothes, which I wore for weeks. My nearest blood, except that which runs in my veins, was shed for liberty. My only brother was shot dead instantly in the Revolution. Liberty is dear to my heart—I cannot endure the thought, that my countrymen should be slaves.

—"Dr. Harris," a veteran of the 1st Rhode Island, in an address to an anti-slavery society in Francestown, New Hampshire, 1842

By 1770, Crispus Attucks, the son of an African father and a Native American mother, had spent some twenty years at sea, having escaped slavery in Framingham, Massachusetts, when he was about twenty-seven years old.

On the night of March 5, 1770, Attucks was in Boston's King Street tavern when an alarm bell was heard from the street's British sentry. When Attucks led a stick- and bat-wielding group of fellows from the tavern, he discovered that the sentry was under "attack" only from snowball-throwing boys. Still, Attucks and his mob took the side of the boys against the Redcoats—using heavy sticks instead of snowballs. Witnesses said that Attucks, striking the first blow, caused arriving British soldiers to open fire. British musket shots hit eleven people, killing five: four white men and Crispus Attucks—the first to die, from two shots to the chest.

Some Bostonians had little regard for the victims. In his defense of the British soldiers, lawyer John Adams blamed Attucks for the mini riot, dismissing him as a rabble-rouser— the leader of a gang of lowlifes and rowdies. The merchant John

Hancock, like Adams a future signer of the Declaration of Independence, also accused Attucks of provoking the "Boston Massacre"—but from a praiseworthy point of view. "Who taught the British soldier that he might be defeated?" Hancock later asked. "Who dared look into his eyes? I place, therefore, this Crispus Attucks in the foremost rank of the men that dared."

Although the British soldiers were acquitted from any wrong-doing, the Americans won the lion's share of public support and sympathy. Crispus Attucks and his companions became the first popular martyrs of the Revolution.

By the time of the Boston Massacre, Britain controlled North America from the Atlantic Ocean to the Mississippi River, as well as most of the islands that made up the West Indies. The debt Britain had incurred securing much of this territory during the French and Indian Wars (1689–1763) led to heavy taxation of the thirteen colonies, which, in British eyes, existed only for the benefit of the mother country. The thirteen colonies, with a budding sense of nationhood, saw any form of taxation as slavery. The mother country's Sugar Act, Stamp Act, and other acts of taxation sparked bold acts of defiance, such as the "Boston Tea Party" on the night of December 16, 1773.

Black people also engaged in protest—against slavery. In 1773, Massachusetts courts and legislature saw several petitions from enslaved blacks, asking for their freedom along with, in one case, some "unimproved land" on which to build new lives. At the time, out of a total population of 2,600,000, in Britain's North American colonies, there were roughly 500,000 black people, with about 460,000 of them enslaved.

Quaker Philadelphia was the heart of early eighteenth-century abolitionism. Benjamin Franklin was among that city's early abolitionists. Anthony Benezet was another. "How many of those who distinguish themselves as Advocates of Liberty remain insensible," Benezet wrote in a 1766 pamphlet, "to the treatment of thousands and tens of thousands of our fellow men, who . . . are at this very time kept in the most deplorable state of slavery."

By the mid-1770s, Boston was the center of abolition as well as revolution. "No country can be called free where there is one slave," declared James Swan, a Boston merchant who had participated in the Boston Tea Party.

"It has always appeared a most iniquitous scheme to me," wrote Abigail Adams in the summer of 1774 to her husband, John, "to fight ourselves for what we are daily robbing and plundering from those who have as good a right to freedom as we have." By "we" Abigail was referring to the American colonies—not the Adams family, for they were not slaveholders. When Abigail wrote this letter, she was at home in Braintree, Massachusetts. John was in Philadelphia, at the First Continental Congress, where representatives from the colonies (except for Georgia) were meeting to discuss their grievances against Britain and ways to get them remedied.

By the spring of 1775, armed revolt seemed the only remedy to many. On March 23, at a convention in Richmond, Virginia, Patrick Henry, a slaveholder, raised the American battle cry with "Give me liberty or give me death!" By then, having anticipated trouble, the British had increased their troops in Boston. These troops were under the command of General Thomas Gage, who was also Royal Governor of Massachusetts.

New England towns and villages had been preparing for war since the winter of 1774. Weapons and gunpowder had been stored. Militiamen were armed and ready, as were Minutemen, an elite militia that could be "ready in a minute" and were organized after the Boston Tea Party. By April 1775, there was a growing number of Patriots ready to do battle against Britain—and against colonists who sided with the mother country, the Loyalists, also known as Tories.

In April 1775, British intelligence learned that a secret meeting in Concord of the illegal Massachusetts Congress had determined to establish an army. On April 18, General Gage ordered troops to proceed to Concord to seize all weapons and ammunition. An advance guard was also sent to Lexington because of similar rumors about an insurrection there.

As British soldiers left by boat across Back Bay late on the night of April 18, two signal lamps ("One if by land, two if by sea") were hung in the steeple of the Old North Church. The printer and silversmith Paul Revere was silently rowed across the Charles River, which was being watched by a heavily armed British warship. Once on shore, Revere mounted one of the fastest horses in the colony to warn first Lexington and then Concord that the British were coming.

In Lexington, Revere, by then joined by two other couriers, was briefly stopped by a British patrol, to whom he supplied "information," with a gun to his head. Armed with Revere's "information," the British patrol told their commanders that at least five hundred Minutemen were waiting on Lexington Green.

The several hundred British soldiers who approached the green early the next morning found a motley army of seventy-seven militiamen. The British Major Pitcairn ordered his troops not to fire and told the Americans to drop their weapons and disperse. Lexington's militia, led by Captain John Parker, was not eager for battle, either. But just as Parker gave the order to withdraw, someone's musket fired (whether American or British is unknown). Scattered shots from both sides followed that first mysterious shot. Eight Americans died and nine were wounded before the shooting stopped.

Prince Easterbrooks, a Lexington slave, was one of the Americans who fought in Captain Parker's company in that first battle of the Revolution—a battle that lasted about fifteen minutes. Easterbrooks was also in the next quick (about five minutes) fight later that same morning: the Battle of Concord.

Entering Concord without resistance at around eight o'clock in the morning, the British found some four hundred Minutemen waiting at North Bridge. There's no mystery as to who fired first here: the British. The Patriots' return fire became known as the "shot heard round the world."

Three British and two Americans were killed before the Americans retreated, with many others from both sides wounded. Prince Easterbrooks, who was among the wounded, was not the only black Massachusetts militiaman defending North Bridge that day. The others included Peter Salem, of Framingham, who had been freed from slavery to enlist; Samuel Craft, of Newton; Caesar Ferrit and his son John, of Natick; and men known only by first names—Pompy, of Braintree (now Quincy), and Prince, of Brookline. Another black Patriot was Lemuel Haynes, who would become the first black ordained Congregational minister in America.

Lemuel Haynes was born in West Hartford, Connecticut,

to a black father and a white mother. At the age of five months, he was indentured to a white farmer (and deacon) of Granville, Massachusetts, who raised him like a son. In 1774, shortly after the end of his indenture, twenty-one-year-old Haynes joined up with the Granville militia. Haynes trained one day a week on the Granville green, learning crude military drills and Native American stealth-fighting techniques, which apparently served him well on that first morning of the Revolution. Shortly after the battles of Lexington and Concord, Haynes penned the poem "The Battle of Lexington," which contains the lines "For Liberty, each Freeman Strives / As [it's] a gift of God / And for it, willing yield their Lives."

Marching back to Boston, the red-coated "victors" of Lexington and Concord—with their heavy and constricting uniforms, plus 60 to 125 pounds of gear—were perfect targets for waiting militiamen. Americans fired at will from behind trees and stone walls at rows of shiny black hats and bright red coats, aiming at officers as well as enlisted men. (Europeans never fired at officers.) "The soldiers were so enraged at suffering from an unseen enemy," wrote a British lieutenant, "that they forced open many of the houses from which the fire proceeded and put to death all those found in them."

Stories of Lexington and Concord describing the Redcoats as savages were sent to England and circulated throughout the colonies. In response to the action at Lexington and Concord, the Congresses of Massachusetts, Connecticut, New Hampshire, and Rhode Island authorized the raising of troops, with Massachusetts pledging the most, close to fourteen thousand.

Among the black men who joined the Patriots' cause shortly after the battles of Lexington and Concord was the freeborn

Barzillai Lew. Like his father, he had seen service in the French and Indian Wars, and his seven generations of descendants would serve America in future wars.

Barzillai Lew was born not far from Boston, in Dracut's "Black North," a black settlement established in 1712. Not long after Barzillai's birth, his parents moved across the Nashua River to Pepperell, where they had three more children. In 1768, Barzillai Lew married Dinah Bowman, a pianist from Lexington whose freedom he bought from her owner, and with whom he'd have many children (all of whom became musicians). When the Revolution broke out, Lew was supporting his family as a cooper.

On May 6, 1775, Lew enlisted as a fifer and drummer in the 27th Massachusetts Regiment. Not long after that, Lew (along with soldier-poet Lemuel Haynes) was among the black men who participated in the raid on the British-held Fort Ticonderoga in upstate New York, on Lake Champlain. The taking of Fort Ticonderoga, under the dual leadership of Benedict Arnold and Ethan Allen, was the first American victory of the war. A month later, Barzillai Lew was once again brave, in the fight that became known as the Battle of Bunker Hill (after the hill the Patriots originally thought would be the site of a big battle).

In the early morning of June 17, 1775, British ships in Boston Harbor opened fire on Breed's Hill, just north of the city, and close to Bunker Hill. The Americans had been fortifying Breed's Hill since late the night before. If the British could be driven from Boston, the Americans would control Massachusetts. With a hundred times as many ships and yet far less manpower than the colonists, the British were trying to destroy the American army.

Despite the bombardment, the Americans, under the command of Colonel William Prescott, continued to fortify their position until late in the afternoon. They then waited behind their parapets for the British to come ashore and storm the hill. Prescott ordered his men to pick out officers and to aim at the crossings of their belts. Anxious about the small stores of ammunition, General Israel Putnam of Connecticut famously added, "Don't fire till you see the whites of their eyes."

After being initially held off in heavy fighting on the beach, the British assaulted Prescott's fort. Rows of Redcoats, led by Major Pitcairn, marched up the hill, firing at intervals but receiving no return fire. When the British were within fifty yards, the Americans finally fired—to devastating effect.

The British fell back, regrouped, and advanced again, marching over their dead and wounded. More British fell in the second advance. By the third advance, the Americans were almost out of ammunition. Offering brief but fierce resistance, they began to retreat as ship-based British marines swarmed over their fortifications.

Major Pitcairn was one of the British officers killed during the battle, and his death is credited to Peter Salem, veteran of Concord. Another black Salem also distinguished himself during the battle—this one Salem Poor, a twenty-eight-year-old free man from Andover, Massachusetts. Poor is credited with the death of another British officer: Lieutenant Colonel James Abercrombie. In December 1775, fourteen American officers would petition the General Court of Massachusetts to ask the Continental Congress to reward Salem Poor. He had "behaved like an Experienced Officer," they stated, "as Well as an Excellent Soldier." There is no record that Poor ever received any reward from the Congress.

Along with Peter Salem and Salem Poor, there were some twenty other black Patriots at the Battle of Bunker Hill, with soldier-fifer Barzillai Lew keeping American morale high by playing "There's Nothing Makes the British Run Like Yankee Doodle Dandy."

Officially a British victory, the battle was nevertheless a boost to the Patriots' morale. It rallied more Americans to join the Patriots' cause—as soldiers and as suppliers of goods and money.

Just before Bunker Hill, the Continental Congress decided to raise an army—the Continental Army—and chose as its commander a six-foot-three, forty-three-year-old delegate from Virginia: the wealthy planter and slaveholder George Washington, a militia leader and veteran of the French and Indian Wars. Washington took command of New England's army of fourteen thousand troops on July 3, 1775, in Cambridge, Massachusetts. He had told his wife that he would be home by Christmas.

Opposition to black soldiers in the Continental Army grew strong soon after George Washington took command: most southern slaveholders were against arming blacks, who would, they feared, set a dangerous example for slaves. In mid-November 1775, Washington was compelled to issue an order that banned the recruitment and reenlistment of black soldiers in the Continental Army.

Around the time that the Continental Army was rejecting black soldiers, the British army was accepting them. On

November 7, 1775, John Murray, Earl of Dunmore, Royal Governor of Virginia, issued a proclamation from Norfolk Harbor inviting able-bodied black men held in slavery by Patriots to join British forces. (Slaves belonging to Tories who answered the call were returned to their masters.) By December 1, 1775, three hundred black men—Lord Dunmore's "Ethiopian Regiment"—were in uniform. Later that month, the regiment was part of the British force defeated by American militiamen at Great Bridge, Virginia. After the battle, the ranks of the Ethiopian Regiment continued to grow, but in the spring and summer of 1776 the regiment was decimated by disease (possibly smallpox). Dunmore wrote that if disease had not killed the Ethiopian Regiment, it would have grown to two thousand men.

Dunmore's proclamation, coupled with the fact that Washington had raised less than half the force needed for his new army, caused the American command to change its mind about black soldiers. In mid-January 1776, the Continental Congress announced that free blacks who had served in the Continental Army could reenlist. Free blacks, as well as slaves substituting for their masters, would fight until the end of the war—a war in which thousands would bleed and die in hundreds more skirmishes and full-blown battles. One of the most famous of these was the Battle of Long Island, which occurred about a month after the Patriots issued their Declaration of Independence.

The first version of the Declaration of Independence contained an anti-slavery statement, which began: "[King George] has waged cruel war against human nature itself, violating its most sacred rights of life and liberty in the persons of a distant people . . . captivating and carrying them into slavery in another hemisphere, or to incur miserable death in their transportation thither." The passage was deleted at the request of South Carolina, Georgia, and New England slave-trading interests.

With the issuance of the Declaration of Independence, white Patriots were not just fighting against Britain: they were fighting for a new nation. So were black Patriots. Inspired by the Declaration, Lemuel Haynes wrote an essay late in 1776, "Liberty Further Extended," in which he declared, "I think it not [an exaggeration] to affirm, that even an African, has Equally as good a right to his Liberty in common with Englishmen . . . consequently, the practice of slave-keeping, which so much abounds in this land is illicit."

In the summer of 1776, Britain's General Sir William Howe was preparing to attack New York. His first goal was to capture Long Island. By August, he was ready to launch the assault.

Washington's army was up against some twenty thousand British and German hired guns (all called Hessians because the majority were from the German principality Hesse-Cassell).

The Battle of Long Island was the most devastating American loss in the early days of the war. Some Hessians bayoneted surrendering Americans and won a reputation as "butchers." The Americans retreated to Brooklyn Heights, having lost fourteen hundred men, many of whom were wounded or captured.

Washington managed to assemble a makeshift fleet of ships. Joining this ragged armada, which gathered in the East River one night in late August to transport troops to lower Manhattan, was Colonel Glover's "Massachusetts Fishermen." There were at least

150 blacks in Glover's regiment of land- and sea-fighting men, the earliest American marines.

The evacuation of men, horses, guns, ammunition, and supplies continued throughout the night. The operation was so quiet that the British never knew what was happening. At dawn, with a sudden fog, Washington stepped into one of the last boats, and the escape (with a third of the army left behind) was accomplished. The British would occupy Manhattan for much of the war, with little complaint from the island's inhabitants because most of them were very pro-British.

The Battle of Long Island was one of a series of defeats for the Continental Army during the summer and early autumn of 1776, and winter was the Revolution's darkest hour.

In November, Washington fell back across New Jersey, plagued by desertions and losses of equipment. By early December he had crossed the Delaware River and into Pennsylvania. It was a time of crisis, but it was also a turning point. After the Battle of Long Island, Washington had formed a strategy to defeat the British. Henceforth, the war would be "defensive," he wrote to Congress. He would "avoid a general action"—he would also, to bedevil the British, "protract the war"—that is, drag out the war by avoiding a lot of quick battles, thereby wearing the British down. Washington was turning retreat into a winning strategy. It was a tactic that would serve him well in Trenton, New Jersey.

The Americans reached Trenton in the dawn of December 26, just as the Hessians stationed there were sleeping off their drunken Christmas celebration. After overrunning the town from two directions, Washington retreated with some 2,400 men—all the men he had left—back across the Delaware River into Pennsylvania. Oliver Cromwell, a twenty-four-year-old New Jersey farmer, was among the blacks who participated in the legendary crossing of the Delaware River, and he would fight in several more battles.

"[We] knocked the British about lively," said Oliver Cromwell in his recollections of the Battle of Princeton, which took place in an orchard outside of this New Jersey town in January 1777. In this battle, a number of British soldiers were captured single-handedly by Primus Hall, a free black Bostonian whose father, Prince Hall, a tanner, made leather drumheads for the Continental Army.

The Patriots had an even greater victory in October 1777, when General John Burgoyne surrendered at Saratoga, the first major British defeat. Discontent, desertion, and a number of suicides among British troops followed, and Hessians deserted heavily. Among the Patriots' black victors of Saratoga was Peter Salem, hero of the Battle of Bunker Hill.

By the end of 1777, blacks had become a familiar part of Washington's army. Salem Poor and Oliver Cromwell were among the black soldiers with him through the encampment at Valley Forge, Pennsylvania, during the grueling winter of 1777–1778.

At Valley Forge there were no battles, but there were plenty of deaths because of a severe shortage of uniforms and supplies. On December 23, 1777, Washington wrote to Congress that 2,900 men were "unfit for duty because they were barefoot and otherwise naked." By February, the number of barefoot and semi-naked had risen to four thousand. The camp ran out of food three times. Men, living in freezing huts, died at the rate of four hundred per month of "putrid fever, the itch, bloody flux or small-pox." As many as 2,500 out of some 10,000 died in six months. Hundreds more deserted for home, or went over to the British.

The Patriots received a great deal of help from abroad. One of their most passionate European supporters was the rich and idealistic Frenchman Marquis de Lafayette, who was at Washington's side at Valley Forge and during several battles. In February 1778, France became the first country to recognize the new American Republic. France also gave the Americans money and military might.

From the French colony Sainte-Domingue (present-day Haiti) came a company of troops called the Fontages Legion (named for their French commander). In the Fontages Legion were several future leaders of the Haitian Revolution. Haiti's future king, twelve-year-old Henri Christophe, a powder boy, was wounded during the ill-fated French-American siege of Savannah of October 1779, in which some seven hundred members of the Fontages Legion participated.

Among the other Europeans who aided the Americans was the Prussian baron Friedrich von Steuben. He gave Americans at Valley Forge their first formal training in the art of war. There was also the Polish engineer Thaddeus Kosciuszko, who, like Lafayette, was an ardent abolitionist. "I would never have drawn my sword in the cause of America," declared Lafayette after the Revolution, "if I could have conceived that thereby I was founding a land of slavery."

Spain entered the war in 1779. Bernardo de Gálvez, governor of the Spanish colony of Louisiana, drove the British from

Louisiana and Alabama. Gálvez mobilized a force of 670 men, which included 80 free blacks of New Orleans, to take Mobile in March 1780. Black men of Louisiana also helped capture Baton Rouge, Louisiana; Pensacola, Florida; and Natchez, Mississippi. Nearly half of Gálvez's Mississippi Valley force was black, among them two companies of Louisiana's black militia. Gálvez turned Louisiana into a vital source of money and supplies for the Americans, shipping them up the Mississippi under the Spanish flag.

As the war dragged on, most states found it increasingly difficult to meet their recruiting quotas. Rhode Island was desperate: its very busy city, Newport, was occupied by British troops, and a blockade was strangling commerce, including the slave trade. Because Newport was the chief slaving port, Rhode Island had the largest population of blacks in New England. And it was in Rhode Island that the first all-black American regiment—the 1st Rhode Island—was formed, in 1778. Colonel Christopher Greene, a native of Rhode Island and one of Washington's best officers, was chosen to command the new 132-man regiment. In February 1778, the Rhode Island legislature announced that any enslaved man who volunteered for the new battalion would be "absolutely free," with the same wages and bounties as regular soldiers.

That August, in the only battle of the Revolution fought in Rhode Island, Hessians directed their main assault against the new black regiment. The 1st Rhode Island held the line against four hours of assaults, thereby helping the American army escape and be ferried to the mainland—another skillfully executed rescue-retreat by the Massachusetts Fishermen. The Americans lost the Battle of Rhode Island, but British casualties were five times greater.

From 1780 until war's end, most of the fighting and dying took place in the South. There, in May 1780, the British had their greatest victory of the war: the taking of Charleston, South Carolina, with the Americans surrendering six thousand soldiers, sailors, and armed citizens, as well as five ships and more than three hundred cannons. Several months later the Continental Army received its sharpest blow, and from one of its own: Benedict Arnold, one of Washington's favorite and best officers, was found out to be a traitor, spying for the British.

Despite these setbacks, the hope of independence burned strong in the hearts of die-hard Patriots. Black soldiers continued to believe that an American victory would mean the end of slavery. Blacks serving in the navy felt likewise.

Hundreds of blacks served in the Continental Navy. A 1775 recruiting poster in Newport, Rhode Island, had sought "ye able backed sailors, men white or black, to volunteer for naval service in ye interest of freedom." Besides doing ordinary seamen duties, blacks in the Continental Navy served as marine sharpshooters and gunmen. (Southern Patriots showed less resistance to black sailors than to black soldiers. Most of the Chesapeake Bay and river pilots of Virginia's navy, for example, were black men who had grown up on the bay or its tributaries.) Joseph Ranger served longer than any other black Virginia seaman. He served on one ship that was blown up by the British navy, and on another whose entire crew was captured and held by the British until the end of the war.

Privateers (private vessels commissioned by a government) were most popular with men who had escaped slavery. But not all blacks who served aboard privateers had been enslaved. Fourteen-year-old James Forten, born free in Philadelphia, signed on in 1781 as a powder boy on the Pennsylvania privateer the *Royal Louis,* under Captain Stephen Decatur, Sr. On Forten's second cruise, the *Royal Louis* (with a crew of two hundred, including twenty blacks) was captured by a British frigate. Black prisoners were usually sold in the West Indies, but Forten (thanks to his talent for shooting marbles) became a playmate of the captain's son. Young Forten was not, however, spared punishment. After he refused to give up his allegiance to America and join the British, he spent the last seven months of the war on the prison ship *Jersey,* a notorious floating disease-ridden dungeon in New York. Prisoners died with such regularity that when British jailers opened the hatches in the morning, their greeting to the men below was "Rebels, turn out your dead!" More than eleven thousand Americans died on the *Jersey.*

At the end of the war, a skeletal Forten, his hair fallen out from malnutrition, was released in the general exchange of prisoners. He walked home barefoot to Philadelphia.

Between January and April 1781, General Cornwallis, the British commander in Virginia, suffered more than fifteen hundred casualties. In September, he found himself besieged by European and American forces at Yorktown, on the Chesapeake Bay in northeastern Virginia. Worn down by smallpox, lack of food, and protracted war, his men were in no condition to put up much of a fight.

Cornwallis dug in at Yorktown with some eight thousand British and Hessian soldiers—against upwards of sixteen thousand troops, the majority of whom were under the command of

George Washington and France's Count Jean de Rochambeau. A smaller contingent was under the command of Friedrich von Steuben and the Marquis de Lafayette. What's more, a French fleet had sailed from the Caribbean to the Chesapeake in early September, just in time to encircle Cornwallis at Yorktown and cut him off from any support by sea.

On the night of October 6, European and American forces stormed the advance British defense post. The British and Hessians were easily overwhelmed. After a week of intense bombardment, Cornwallis's officers told him that he owed it to his men to surrender.

At the Yorktown surrender ceremony, on October 19, 1781, British and Hessian soldiers were well uniformed, as were the French officers and troops. Most of the Americans, however, were ragged, and many were barefoot. Thanks to their rich patrons, the 1st Rhode Island Regiment was one of the few American units in full uniform.

"The war over, and peace restored, these men returned to their respective states," wrote American army surgeon William Eustis, future governor of Massachusetts, "and who could have said to them, on their return to civil life, after having shed their blood in common with whites in the defense of the liberties of the country: 'You are not to participate in the rights secured by the struggle, or in the liberty for which you have been fighting.'" Eustis was writing of the 1st Rhode Island, but his words could have referred to any black soldier or sailor.

The American Revolution continued to exist in name only, without fighting, for another year. On April 19, 1783, it officially ended, eight years to the day after the battles of Lexington and Concord. The peace was formally signed in Paris that September. On November 25, the British army and navy began to evacuate New York City. General Washington was home for Christmas, eight years later than he had planned.

Thousands of blacks who had escaped slavery or had been freed during the war went looking for new homes. A great number accepted the British offer of free transport to Britain or its colonies. As for the blacks who remained in America, many veterans had trouble getting pensions, as well as their promised freedom. Gad Asher, a substitute for his East Guilford, Connecticut, owner, won his. Asher's 1783 disability pension called him "unfit for any further duty, either in the field, or in garrison, being blind." Gad Asher could no longer fight, but he could still inspire.

Gad Asher's grandson, Jeremiah Asher, would one day write that his grandfather's war stories almost made him believe that he "had more rights than any white man in the town." Asher, a Baptist minister who would serve in the Civil War as a Union Army chaplain, also drew strength from the recollections of other black veterans of the Revolution. "Thus, my first ideas of the right of the colored man to life, liberty and the pursuit of happiness were received from these old veterans and champions for liberty."

In June 1782, America had taken as its motto *"E pluribus unum"*—"Out of many, one." Some Americans, New Englanders especially, thought the "one" included blacks. Vermont had abolished slavery in 1777. In 1784, Massachusetts did the same, and Connecticut and Rhode Island passed gradual emancipation acts.

Several slaveholders in the South renounced slavery. "[Keeping] fellow men in . . . slavery is repugnant to the golden law of God and the unalienable right of mankind as well as to every principle of the late glorious revolution," wrote Philip Graham of Maryland, who freed his slaves in 1787.

Hopes that the new nation would abolish slavery were dashed in the summer of 1787 at the Constitutional Convention in Philadelphia. The South had threatened to secede if slavery was abolished throughout America. The South's devotion to slavery intensified with the introduction, in 1793, of the cotton gin, which sped up the processing of raw cotton and thus fueled the growth of more and larger cotton plantations. These plantations would be far more profitable if worked by slave instead of paid labor. Also in 1793 came the Fugitive Slave Law, which declared that runaways could be seized in any state and returned to their owners on the owner's word alone (which meant free blacks could—and would— be kidnapped and enslaved). This new law also made it a crime to harbor people who escaped slavery or to prevent their arrest. Yet another important event of 1793 was the abolition of slavery in Upper Canada (present-day Ontario). Consequently, many who escaped slavery made Canada their final destination.

At the dawn of the nineteenth century, 90 percent of America's roughly 1 million blacks—close to 19 percent of the population— were in bondage. As slavery continued, so did escapes and uprisings, such as the one masterminded by Gabriel Prosser, a twenty-four-year-old blacksmith. Prosser's goal was to create an independent nation within Virginia. Eventually, he recruited more than a thousand enslaved people from at least three counties around Richmond. He made the veterans of the Revolution among them group leaders.

On Saturday night, August 30, 1800, Prosser assembled his followers at a brook on his owner's property and readied them to march on Richmond, about six miles away. Richmond was short on men and muskets—the surprise attack might have succeeded—but the plan was doomed by nature and by human treachery. Before Prosser's troops could attack, there was a sudden heavy rainstorm, washing out all roads and bridges to Richmond, where Governor James Monroe's Virginia militia was waiting. Two black people, both enslaved, had informed. About three dozen insurrectionists, including Prosser, were eventually hanged. Other uprisings would be planned and other uprisings would be suppressed, as happened in Louisiana in 1811.

It was in early January 1811 that Charles Deslondes, a free man from Haiti, led a rebellion of more than four hundred enslaved people outside New Orleans. Deslondes's troops destroyed several plantations and killed at least two white people, including the son of Major Andry, the owner of the plantation where the uprising began. The rebels fled to the woods, where Andry's posse followed and summarily executed any they captured. The next day, Governor William Claiborne called out troops to hunt down more of the rebels. These troops included the battalion of New Orleans's black militia, the group that had helped Bernardo de Gálvez drive the British from the lower Mississippi during the Revolution. This corps would also prove useful to America in the War of 1812.

THE WAR OF 1812

Her first broadside killed two men and wounded six others. . . . The name of one of my poor fellows who was killed ought to be registered in the book of fame, and remembered with reverence as long as bravery is considered a virtue; he was a black man by the name of John Johnson; a 24 lb. shot struck him in the hip and took away all the lower part of his body. . . .

The other was also a black man, by the name of John Davis, and was struck in much the same way: he fell near me, and several times requested to be thrown overboard, saying, he was only in the way of others.

—Nathaniel Shaler, commander of the privateer schooner *Governor Tompkins*, recalling a battle with a British ship on January 1, 1813

By 1812, America had doubled in size. In 1783, in the Treaty of Paris, Britain had ceded to America the Northwest Territory, much of which is what we today call the Midwest. America had gained more territory, through the Louisiana Purchase of 1803, following France's repeated failures to crush the independence struggle of its colony Sainte-Domingue, which resulted in the first black republic in the Western Hemisphere: Haiti. Soured on the Americas, at the rock-bottom price of four cents an acre (total purchase price: $15 million), France sold its huge chunk of land that stretched, east to west, from the Mississippi River to the Rocky Mountains, and, north to south, from Canada to the Gulf of Mexico. America's desire to hold on to its new lands and to expand was a factor in the War of 1812 between America and Britain, ostensibly fought for freedom of the seas.

America's chief complaints against Britain were interference with American shipping and naval impressment (forcing men into the Royal Navy). For some time, British sailors had been escaping the terrible conditions of their service and fleeing to American ships (although these were only slightly better). In response, Britain claimed the right to stop all neutral vessels on the high seas and remove sailors of British birth, impressing them into service—but too many Americans were taken by "mistake."

The roots of war lay in Britain's ongoing conflict with France. After Admiral Lord Horatio Nelson's celebrated defeat of the French at the Battle of Trafalgar in 1805, France had tried to stop British trade with the rest of continental Europe. The British had retaliated by blockading French ports. British and French blockades had a disastrous effect on American shipping, prompting complaints to both sides.

Tensions increased in 1808, when a British warship outside Norfolk, Virginia, fired on the U.S. frigate *Chesapeake* because its captain had refused to let his ship be searched. Three American sailors were killed, eighteen wounded, and four seized as deserters from the British navy. Three of the so-called deserters were black Americans, and although they were released, President Thomas Jefferson nevertheless ordered all British vessels out of his nation's harbors.

A war between America and Britain was of great advantage to France. Seeking to woo America to the French side, Napoleon exempted America from all French shipping restrictions in 1810. The following year, although Britain apologized for the *Chesapeake* incident and paid damages, President James Madison shut off all British trade. He eventually asked Congress for a declaration of war, which Congress issued on June 18, 1812, even though Britain had announced two days earlier that it would repeal the shipping and impressment laws.

War with Britain had been bitterly contested between anti-war New Englanders, called Doves, and pro-war Southerners and Westerners, called Hawks.

"Is the rod of British power to be forever suspended over our heads?" asked Representative Henry Clay of Kentucky. Clay preferred expansion to peace, as did many other Southerners and Westerners. Southerners wanted the Spanish (British allies at the time) out of Florida. Westerners wanted the British out of western Canada.

New England opposed the war partly out of loyalty to Britain and opposition to Napoleon, but mostly because war would completely destroy the American shipping industry. Some New Englanders even talked of secession—forming a separate nation out of the thirteen original colonies and negotiating a separate peace with Britain.

Unlike most New Englanders, the former revolutionary John Adams, who had served as America's first vice president and second president, was a Hawk. Adams believed that war against Britain was "necessary to convince France that we are something; and above all necessary to convince ourselves, that we are not-Nothing."

When the war broke out, the U.S. treasury was nearly empty. While the War Department had been authorized to recruit fifty thousand one-year volunteers, it managed to obtain only ten thousand men. Britain had a thousand fighting ships, with more than a hundred battleships; America had no battleship-class vessels, and only seventeen frigates and sloops-of-war. But the British were in for a surprise. Three American frigates, the

Constitution (nicknamed Old Ironsides), the *President,* and the *United States,* were faster, and had heavier broadsides—all the better to withstand cannon shot—than any ship of their class in the world.

One-sixth of the U.S. Navy seamen who served on warships and privateers during the war were black. They fought conspicuously in the only two American naval victories that directly affected the course of the war and permitted American inroads into Canada. One of these was Captain Oliver Hazard Perry's victory on Lake Erie, on September 10, 1813.

Over a hundred blacks were among the four hundred men in Perry's 1813 Great Lakes Armada, dispatched to spearhead an invasion of Canada. Perry's Lake Erie victory forced the British to pull out of Detroit, and much of what is now Michigan came under American control. This allowed Major General William Henry Harrison to cross Lake Michigan and defeat the retreating British at Canada's Battle of the Thames. (By 1814, however, Napoleon had lost in Europe and the British were able to send new troops to Canada, thus ending America's hopes of Canadian conquest.)

Britain's navy had black sailors, too. Britain's Rear Admiral George Cockburn organized a hard-fighting unit of runaway slaves, known as the Black Marines. In August, the Black Marines were part of the fifteen-hundred-member British invading force in Bladensburg, Maryland. It was a humiliating American defeat: some five thousand Virginia and Maryland soldiers ran away, terrified by the sight and sound of the new British rockets. Fortunately for national honor, six hundred sailors and marines from a gunboat flotilla (with several blacks among them) stayed with their guns.

A few days after Bladensburg, the Black Marines were in the British advance that captured Washington, D.C. President James Madison and his wife, Dolley, had been forced to evacuate. The Capitol Building was burned, and the President's House (as the White House was called) was looted before it was torched.

Americans had their revenge a month later, when they defeated the British at the Battle of Baltimore.

While America's navy welcomed blacks into its ranks, its army, for the most part, did not. Most states abided by the 1792 congressional act that restricted militia service to "free able-bodied white male citizens." The exceptions included New York, which organized two regiments of approximately two thousand blacks, enslaved and free, promising freedom to the former at the end of the war. Another exception was found in Louisiana.

With the outbreak of the war, Louisiana's Governor William Claiborne had written to President Madison about the past valor of New Orleans's black militia. Shortly thereafter, the Louisiana military began recruiting free blacks.

The new Battalion of Free Men of Color was organized around the earlier militia group. The law specified that all militia officers be white, but there were three black second lieutenants: Isidore Honoré, Vincent Populus, and Joseph Savary.

In the autumn of 1814, General Andrew Jackson, who had retaken Pensacola, Florida, from the British and was defending

Mobile, Alabama, was called to save New Orleans from imminent invasion. Writing to Jackson, Governor Claiborne again lobbied for the use of New Orleans's black militia.

On September 21, 1814, Jackson issued a proclamation, calling on Louisiana's "free men of color" to "take up" arms. "To every noble-hearted, generous, freeman of color, volunteering to serve during the present contest with Great Britain, and no longer," said Jackson, "there will be paid the same bounty, in money and lands, now received by the white soldiers of the U[nited] States." This bounty was 160 acres of land and $124 in cash. The men who answered the call would be segregated.

Britain's Major General Pakenham's invasion armada was gathering in Jamaica and preparing to move on New Orleans as Second Lieutenant Isidore Honoré's new battalion reported to duty on December 12, 1814.

On December 18, Jackson addressed his six thousand troops, some five hundred of whom were free blacks. A special address was read to the black men. In it, Jackson stated that "the President of the United States shall be informed of your conduct on the present occasion, and the voice of the representatives of the American Nation shall applaud your valor, as your General now praises your ardor." The Battle of New Orleans began on December 23, 1814.

Jackson had misjudged the British. Thinking they would come in overland, he sent the black battalions to join in guarding the vulnerable route from Mobile. When he discovered that the British had come by water, through the bayous, and were now encamped nine miles outside the city, he ordered a night assault.

The fighting was fierce. Savary's young drummer boy, Jordan Noble, beating nonstop "in the hottest hell of fire," was the rallying point in the dark for the black troops. Savary himself could be heard above the battle, shouting out, "March on! March on, my friends, march on against the enemies of the country!" Jackson, praising Savary's troops for "great bravery," was said to have hugged him on the battlefield.

The British were held off, and all New Orleans men were called to help fortify Rodriguez Canal, on the right bank of the Mississippi. When the British finally marched on the city, on January 8, they met a fortified line on the Chalmette Plains, opposite the canal—and the largest black force ever seen in America. The two black battalions stood side by side in the middle of this "Jackson Line," and black soldiers were scattered throughout the other regiments.

At battle's end, one-third of the wounded were from the black battalions, and included Sergeant Belton Savary, Major Savary's brother, who died two days after the battle. The British lost two thousand men, including General Pakenham. "I have always believed," Jackson later wrote to President Monroe, "[that Pakenham] fell from the bullet of a free man of color, who was a famous rifle shot."

"The two corps of colored volunteers have not disappointed the hopes that were formed of their courage and perseverance in the performance of their duty," said Jackson shortly after the battle. He singled out Joseph Savary for special mention.

Meanwhile, a furious Savary defied a post-battle order forbidding blacks to join in the victory parade, and marched his men through the city. Most of the other free men of color who fought in New Orleans were also soon disillusioned, regarding themselves as *objets de mépris* (objects of contempt) in the eyes of white society. Although a few of these men (or their descendants) won pensions, it is doubtful that any received their promised bounty.

The Battle of New Orleans was the worst British military defeat since the Revolution and a psychological high point for America. Ironically, this triumph came after the war was technically over: on December 24, 1814, representatives of America and Britain had signed a peace treaty in Ghent, Belgium. (In pre-telegraph days, news traveled very slowly.)

The Revolution had given America independence and a national identity; the War of 1812 gave it a place in the larger world—proving, in John Adams's words, that America was "not nothing."

Both Britain and America ultimately saw the war as wasteful, and both could claim victory. The Treaty of Ghent specified that all lands captured by either side were to be returned. Everything would be almost exactly as it was before the war. The treaty also mandated that blacks who fled to the British be returned to their masters or sold in the West Indies, with compensation to American owners.

In the aftermath of the war, free blacks (approximately 200,000 in a total population of about 10 million) became a beleaguered group. In northern cities, they had to compete with immigrants for employment; in the South, they were perceived as a threat to slavery. Many whites felt that America would be better off without free blacks.

Late in 1816, the Southerners Bushrod Washington and John Randolph were among the founders of the American Colonization Society (ACS). At the first meeting, Henry Clay, still a member of Congress, praised the society's aim "to rid our country of a useless and pernicious, if not dangerous portion of its population—the free Negro." The ACS eventually purchased territory near Cape Mesurado, on the West African coast, for the resettlement of freeborn and freed blacks. The ACS named the colony Liberia. Some blacks thought emigration to Africa a good thing. The majority, however, did not.

In January 1817, three thousand blacks met in Philadelphia, at Richard Allen's church, Bethel, to protest the work of the ACS. Among the leaders of the meeting was a veteran of the Revolution, the very successful sailmaker James Forten.

This assembly of free blacks affirmed their right and desire to remain in America, asserting that "any measure . . . having a tendency to banish us from her bosom, would not only be cruel, but in direct violation of those principles, which have been the boast of this republic." Among their resolutions—"that we never will separate ourselves voluntarily from the slave population in this country; they are our brethren by the ties of consanguinity, of suffering, and of wrong."

Hostility toward free blacks only continued. For one, in 1820, the U.S. government announced: "No Negro or Mulatto will be received as a recruit of the Army."

Blacks could not be American soldiers, but they could still wage war—on slavery. Some did so by plotting insurrections, as

Denmark Vesey, a carpenter in Charleston, South Carolina, did in December 1821. (The plot was undone, however, in May 1822, when two slaves betrayed it.) Other blacks waged war against slavery through nonviolent means. Chief among such abolitionists was Frederick Douglass, who had escaped bondage in Maryland in 1838. After his escape, Douglass fought against slavery not only in his lectures and his newspaper articles, but also as a worker on the Underground Railroad.

With the help of more than 3,000 black and white Railroad members, an estimated 75,000 children and adults escaped slavery in the 1850s alone. Most runaways traveled one of the two main lines: along the eastern seaboard to Canada, or through Kentucky into Ohio. "Station masters," "chief engineers," and "conductors" led fugitives north. Without a doubt the most celebrated conductor was the woman who escaped captivity in Maryland in 1849: Harriet Tubman. Between 1851 and 1860, Tubman helped more than three hundred people make their way to freedom in the "Promised Land" (Canada).

Another legendary abolitionist was the white Bostonian William Lloyd Garrison, who published the first edition of his newspaper, *The Liberator*, on New Year's Day 1831, with James Forten among the newspaper's staunchest benefactors. Garrison believed that abolitionists should neither vote nor run for office in a country where slavery was legal, and he publicly burned the U.S. Constitution. "No compromise with slavery! No union with slaveholders!" he thundered.

Frederick Douglass, who regarded *The Liberator* as "second only to the Bible," expressed "love" for the newspaper and its editor. It was with Garrison's American Anti-Slavery Society that Douglass became a star lecturer. But Douglass and Garrison eventually had a falling out over Garrison's opposition to war. By the late 1850s, Douglass believed in voting, running for office, and, if necessary, waging real war for the liberation of the millions of children and adults enslaved in America. And war was what it took to rid the nation of slavery.

THE CIVIL WAR

Once let the black man get upon his person the brass letters, U.S., let him get an eagle on his buttons, and a musket on his shoulder and bullets in his pocket, and there is no power on earth which can deny that he has earned the right to citizenship in the United States.

—Frederick Douglass, 1863

"**A** house divided against itself cannot stand. I believe this government cannot endure, permanently half *slave* and half *free*," declared the Republican Party's Abraham Lincoln during his 1858 Illinois Senate campaign against the Democratic Party's Stephen Douglas. "I do not expect the house to fall," Lincoln continued, "but I do expect it will cease to be divided. It will become all *one* thing, or all the *other*." Lincoln did not win that Senate race, but he went on to become the Republican Party's candidate in the upcoming presidential election.

In November 1860, Lincoln became the sixteenth president of the United States of America. It was an America with roughly four million people—one out of every seven—enslaved. And it was an America about to be torn asunder.

Tensions between pro-slavery and anti-slavery Americans had been intensifying since the Missouri Compromise of 1820, which prohibited slavery in territory in the Louisiana Purchase north of the Ohio River (except for Missouri).

The Compromise of 1850 was another cause of friction. In 1848, at the end of the Mexican-American War (sparked by America's claim on Texas), America came into possession of a huge amount of territory in the West (present-day California, Arizona, Nevada, and Utah, and parts of New Mexico, Colorado, and Wyoming). The South, which had supported war in the belief that slavery would be allowed in any new territory gained, was furious when California asked to enter the Union as a free state. To prevent full-scale conflict, a compromise was carved out. California would be free and slave trading, though not slave-holding, would be abolished in the nation's capital. In exchange, the New Mexico and Utah territories would be without restrictions on slavery.

The Compromise of 1850 also contained a new Fugitive Slave Act, which permitted an alleged runaway to be seized anywhere in the U.S.; denied a trial by jury; forbidden to testify or summon witnesses on his or her behalf; and sent south no matter how long he or she had been free. It was an open invitation to kidnap black people—and it prompted more Northerners to join the anti-slavery campaign.

The 1850s also saw the Kansas-Nebraska Act, which allowed settlers in these two territories to decide whether or not to prohibit slavery there. This act, which nullified the Missouri Compromise, outraged many Northerners, and led to "Bleeding Kansas": the eruption of violence in May 1856 between pro-slavery and anti-slavery forces, which lasted for several years. (In the end, Kansas entered the Union as a free state in 1861, the same year that slavery was abolished in Nebraska, which became a state after the Civil War.) Among the other milestones on the road to civil war was John Brown's Raid on Harpers Ferry.

Intent on starting an uprising that would sweep south, on October 16, 1859, John Brown, a veteran of "Bleeding Kansas," led his "army" of seventeen white men (including three of his sons) and five black men in an assault on the U.S. arsenal at Harpers Ferry, Virginia (now West Virginia). The raid had been financed by prominent Boston abolitionists known as "The Secret Six."

Leading the troops who suppressed the rebellion were two future officers of the Confederacy: Colonel Robert E. Lee and Lieutenant J.E.B. Stuart. Only one of John Brown's Raiders survived: a black man, Osborne Anderson, who escaped to Canada (and later served in the Union Army). Most of Brown's men were killed in the armory. Others, including John Brown, were jailed, tried, and hanged. John Brown became the anti-slavery movement's great martyr. Even the pacifist William Lloyd Garrison called it "High Noon" and wished "success to every slave insurrection at the South."

For many in the South, the election of Abraham Lincoln to the presidency was the last straw. On December 20, 1860, South Carolina, unable to accept a president and a party "whose opinions and purposes are hostile to slavery," declared itself an "independent commonwealth." By early February 1861, Alabama, Florida, Georgia, Louisiana, Mississippi, and Texas had declared their independence. That same month, the Confederate States of America (CSA) was established. Former U.S. Senator Jefferson Davis of Mississippi became its president.

Calling slavery the "immediate cause" of secession, CSA Vice President Alexander Stephens, a former congressional representative from Georgia, announced in March 1861 that the "cornerstone" of the Confederacy was the idea that "the negro is not equal to the white man" and that slavery is "his natural and normal condition."

Lincoln was always sensitive to pro-slavery border states that remained in the Union (Delaware, Kentucky, Maryland, and

Missouri), and thus he insisted that the issue was preservation of the Union, not slavery.

"If we aint fightin' fer slavery then I'd like to know what we are fightin' fer" was the succinct response of Nathan Bedford Forrest, a Tennessee slave trader and future Confederate general. Forrest seemed to speak for the majority of Southerners—a host of whom cheered when Confederate forces fired on Union-held Fort Sumter in the harbor of Charleston, South Carolina, on April 12, 1861.

Following this "first shot" of the Civil War, four more states joined the CSA: Arkansas, North Carolina, Tennessee, and Virginia, with Richmond, Virginia, becoming the Confederate capital.

At the outset of the war, the Union saw no need for blacks in its military. In contrast, the Confederacy used blacks from the beginning as military laborers. "Slave labor was so important to the southern war effort," James M. McPherson wrote in his book *Battle Cry of Freedom*, "that the government impressed slaves into service before it began drafting white men as soldiers."

The Union decided to use blacks in the military in July 1861, following the huge defeat in the first Battle of Bull Run (Manassas Junction, Virginia). After Bull Run, President Lincoln called for fifty thousand blacks to serve in the Union Army in a variety of capacities, including as medical assistants, engineers, laborers, longshoremen, blacksmiths, carpenters, masons, laundresses, scouts, servants, and spies—but not as soldiers.

"Colored men were good enough to fight under [George] Washington," Frederick Douglass complained. "They are not good enough to fight under McClellan." (General George B.

McClellan, appointed Union general-in-chief in November, insisted that his armies return runaway slaves to their masters.) Some Union generals thought blacks "good enough" to fight early on in the war. Major General John C. Frémont was one. In August 1861, following passage of the First Confiscation Act, which declared that all enslaved people used to support the Confederate military were free, Frémont issued a proclamation from Missouri that all enslaved people who took up arms for the Union would be free. Lincoln was so furious that he fired Frémont (but later reinstated him). Meanwhile, in the Southeast, Union success prompted another general to raise black troops.

The Union Navy, in which blacks were already serving under integrated conditions, but with no rank higher than Boy (the lowest), had taken control of the major waterways, north and south, early in the war. In November 1861, black sailors were part of Commander Samuel F. DuPont's Union armada when it captured Port Royal Island and the adjacent South Carolina Sea Islands, some fifty miles southwest of Charleston.

In the spring of 1862, with fewer than eleven thousand men to hold the South Carolina, Georgia, and Florida coasts, General David Hunter began raising a regiment of escapees from slavery in South Carolina. Hunter's regiment was short-lived, however. President Lincoln killed it.

It was also in the spring of 1862, in May, that the pilot of the armed Confederate dispatch boat the *Planter* became a Union hero when he stole the ship from the dock while its white officers and crew were ashore. This man was Robert Smalls, who had been born in slavery in Beaufort, South Carolina.

After spiriting his wife and two children and five other black people aboard the *Planter*, Smalls sailed out of Charleston

Harbor. Once the *Planter* was in sight of Union blockade ships, the white flag of truce went up. Smalls received a substantial financial reward from the U.S. Congress and was made captain of the *Planter* when it was refitted as a gunboat. After the war, Smalls became a member of the U.S. Congress.

The year 1862 had opened with Union victories. In January, the Union Army and Navy forces had captured New Orleans. The Army was victorious again in February in Tennessee, led by the electrifying General Ulysses S. Grant. April brought the Battle of Shiloh, a bloody stalemate—but the North claimed victory because it cleared Confederate troops out of Tennessee and began the process of dividing the Confederacy at the Mississippi River.

The Battle of Shiloh was known as a "soldier's battle" because of the seemingly poor leadership on both sides. General Grant was rumored to have been drunk. "I can't spare this man—he fights!" was Lincoln's reply to demands for Grant's dismissal after Shiloh. Grant's aggressiveness was in direct contrast to the timidity of Union General-in-Chief George McClellan (who would be relieved of command that fall).

In July 1862, Lincoln signed the Second Confiscation Act. This act declared that slaves held by people supporting the Confederates would be free upon coming into Union lines or territory under Union control. The act gave the president power to "employ" blacks for the suppression of rebellion. In August, the repercussions began. Without Lincoln's approval, General Benjamin Butler called for black volunteers in newly captured New Orleans. The response was the French-speaking 1st Regiment of Louisiana Native Guards, many of whose grandfathers had fought in the War of 1812.

It was also in August that David Hunter's short-lived corps of South Carolina troops was born anew, when General Rufus Saxton was allowed to organize the 1st South Carolina Volunteers, to be based on St. Helena. The 1st South Carolina was the first official Union Army regiment of escapees from slavery. This regiment's colonel was an abolitionist: writer and cleric Thomas Wentworth Higginson, formerly captain of the 51st Massachusetts Infantry and one of the "Secret Six" who had funded John Brown's raid. A month after the birth of the 1st Louisiana and the 1st South Carolina, Brigadier James H. Lane formed the 1st Kansas Colored Volunteers, calling on people enslaved in Missouri and Arkansas to flee to Kansas and fight for the Union. In October 1862, the 1st Kansas became the first black regiment of the Civil War to actually engage in combat, holding off a superior force of rebel guerrillas near Butler, Missouri.

In September 1862, President Lincoln had made a stupendous and long-awaited announcement: all people held in slavery in rebel states would be freed on January 1, 1863.

"If my name ever goes into history, it will be for this act," said Lincoln on New Year's Eve 1862, when he signed the Emancipation Proclamation. It was an act "sincerely believed to be an act of justice, warranted by the Constitution, upon military necessity" on which Lincoln invoked "the considerate judgment of mankind, and the gracious favor of Almighty God."

The Emancipation Proclamation left about 800,000 people in slavery in territory loyal to the Union (West Virginia, parts of eastern Virginia, and thirteen parishes of Louisiana). But given that it freed more than 3 million people, it is understandable that, to the world at large, and especially to most black people, blacks in America were at last "forever free." What's more, blacks would be allowed in greater numbers to defend that liberty on the battlefield: "And I further declare and make known," Lincoln wrote near the end of the Proclamation, "that [blacks] of suitable condition, will be received into the armed service of the United States."

Swift on the heels of the Emancipation Proclamation, Boston abolitionists created the 54th Massachusetts, the first northern black volunteer regiment.

Frederick Douglass was among the most passionate recruiters for the 54th, raising volunteers in his travels (from Boston to St. Louis, Missouri) and in his newspaper. "Men of Color, to Arms!" was the headline of one address. Two of Douglass's sons, Charles and Lewis, were the first to enlist from New York, with Lewis becoming the 54th's first sergeant major.

The 54th received terrific support from a group of prominent white Bostonians known as the Massachusetts Black Committee. Organized by Massachusetts Governor John A. Andrew and Major George Stearns (another Secret Sixer), the Black Committee raised $100,000 for regimental expenses. Several Black Committee members' sons became officers in the 54th. And when it came to white officers, Governor Andrew was looking for men "of military experience, of firm antislavery principles, ambitious, superior to vulgar contempt for color, and having faith in the capacity of colored men for military service."

The soldier who would be the 54th's leader certainly fit the bill. He was twenty-five-year-old Captain Robert Gould Shaw, the only son of a Black Committee member. Shaw had seen combat. He was an ardent abolitionist. And he was very much in favor of the Union using black soldiers. "Isn't it extraordinary," Shaw had written a family friend in 1861, "that the Government won't make use of the instrument that would finish the war sooner than anything else—[namely] the slaves? What a lick it would be to them, to call all the blacks in the country to come and enlist in our army!"

"Wanted. Good men for the Fifty-Fourth Regiment of Massachusetts Volunteers of African Descent, Col. Robert G. Shaw [commanding]," read the notice "To Colored Men," in *The Boston Journal*. It offered "$100 bounty at expiration of term of service. Pay $13 per month, and State aid for families." Good men did indeed respond to notices such as this, but the best of them would not be allowed to serve up to their potential. The Union Army had a very restrictive policy toward black officers. The 54th was permitted two black chaplains, its only black officers: William Jackson and Samuel Harrison.

One member of this regiment, Captain Luis F. Emilio, who was from Salem and of Portuguese descent, wrote a history of the 54th, *A Brave Black Regiment*. "Only a small proportion had been slaves," Emilio wrote of the black men who enlisted in the 54th. The regiment represented a cross section of black middle-class and working-class America. They were farmers, laborers, seamen, clerks, barbers, cooks, machinists, printers, blacksmiths, butlers, brickmakers, carpenters, dentists, and pharmacists. They came from Maine, Connecticut, Vermont, New Hampshire, Rhode Island, New York, Pennsylvania, Ohio, Michigan, Illinois, Indiana, Kentucky, Missouri, Maryland, South Carolina, Canada, the Caribbean—and, of course, from Massachusetts.

The 54th did nothing but grow. In late May 1863, the regiment would have a sister regiment, the 55th Massachusetts. One of its members was Zimri Lew, a great-grandson of a veteran of the Revolution, Barzillai Lew.

By March 1863, Abraham Lincoln had grown more confident about the use of black soldiers. "The bare sight of 50,000 armed and drilled black soldiers upon the banks of the Mississippi would end the rebellion at once," Lincoln wrote to Andrew Johnson, who was both a slaveholder and the military governor of Union-controlled Tennessee. That same month, to the horror of the South, the 1st and 2nd South Carolina Volunteers captured Jacksonville, Florida.

In May 1863, as the Union began a major southern offensive, the U.S. War Department's General Order 143 permitted blacks to enlist officially in the Union Army. They would belong to one central body: the United States Colored Troops (USCT). All black troops, except for state-sponsored regiments—one new Connecticut unit, the 54th, 55th, and the new 5th Massachusetts Cavalry—were absorbed into the USCT.

While rejecting the idea of black officers for black troops, the U.S. War Department was extremely particular about the white officers it chose to lead them. Nine thousand whites applied for officer commissions in the USCT; only a quarter of that number received them. Some applied because they sought higher rank, or better pay, but many had abolitionist sympathies.

Hearing a fifteen-year-old boy who had escaped slavery describe his life in bondage, a white soldier of the 70th Indiana volunteered to join the USCT out of a newly born animosity toward Southerners. "To hear this child tell about the thrashing he has received from his brutal master and the chains and weights he has carried in the field," the white soldier wrote, "is enough to make a man feel like it would be in God's service to shoot them down like buzzards." A fair number of Southerners felt the same way about white officers of black troops. Back in August 1862, the Confederacy had branded black troops and their white officers "outlaws." On May 1, 1863, the Confederate Congress issued another directive against white officers of black troops: they would be treated as inciters of servile rebellion and, if captured, would be "put to death, or otherwise punished." The Confederate general and ex–slave trader Nathan Bedford Forrest offered $1,000 for the head of "a commander of a nigger regiment."

The first major engagement for black troops occurred in the May 1863 siege of Port Hudson, Louisiana, for control of the Mississippi River. The first assault, on May 27, although not a Union victory, was a victory for black soldiers. Captain André Cailloux's 1st Louisiana had asked to lead the attack, charging six times over open ground under heavy artillery fire. Cailloux was killed on the last charge as, already wounded, he waved his sword, shouting, *"Suivez-moi!"* ("Follow me!")

"You have no idea how my prejudices with regard to negro troops have been dispelled by the battle," a white officer wrote home to his family. "The brigade of negroes behaved magnificently and fought splendidly. . . . They are far superior in discipline to the white troops and just as brave."

In early June, USCT soldiers once again proved themselves brave when they beat back a rebel assault in hand-to-hand combat at Milliken's Bend, a Union outpost just above Vicksburg,

Mississippi. The 5th USCT Heavy Artillery lost nearly 45 percent of its men—the highest proportion of deaths suffered by a single regiment during the entire war.

A few days before the battle at Milliken's Bend, the 54th Massachusetts headed off to war. They had been ordered to report to General David Hunter at Hilton Head, South Carolina.

Progressive Bostonians celebrated the 54th mightily. "All along the route the sidewalks, windows, and balconies were thronged with spectators, and the appearance of the regiment caused repeated cheers and waving of flags and handkerchiefs," wrote Luis F. Emilio of the 54th's farewell parade on May 28, 1863.

On June 3, the 54th marched through Beaufort, South Carolina. The regiment had arrived in time to hear the bad news that black troops would be paid seven dollars a month, not the promised thirteen. Shaw refused to have the regiment paid at all. The men should either be discharged "or receive the full pay which was promised them," he said. The Massachusetts legislature offered to make up the difference; but the regiment refused, and would fight without pay for more than a year. (Black combat troops would not begin to receive equal pay until September 1864.)

Despite the salary battle, the 54th's morale was high that summer. The "high tide of the Confederacy" had already begun to recede in the wake of the Battle of Gettysburg (Pennsylvania) in early July, which resulted in more than twenty thousand Union and Confederate casualties. Moreover, the Union continued to gain control of the Mississippi River.

On July 4, the day of General Robert E. Lee's retreat from Gettysburg, the battle-scarred 1st Louisiana participated in the fall of Vicksburg, the last Confederate stronghold on the Mississippi. Men of the 54th saw action less than two weeks later: on South Carolina's James Island, rescuing Connecticut troops from certain capture. In relieving the 10th Connecticut, fourteen members of the 54th were killed. Immediately after the battle, the survivors trooped to nearby Morris Island.

About a mile and a half from Fort Sumter, Morris Island was the site of Fort Wagner, the last defense of Charleston. When Shaw landed on Morris Island in the late afternoon of July 18, General George C. Strong informed him that the 54th and 6th Massachusetts, along with troops from several other regiments, would storm Fort Wagner that night. Two earlier Union attacks had failed, with 339 Union casualties to the Confederates' 12.

"You may lead the column if you say yes," Strong said. "Your men, I know are worn out, but do as you choose."

The 54th had gone three days without rest and twenty-four hours without food. Nevertheless, Shaw said yes, having no idea what his troops would be up against. Major General Quincy Adams Gillmore (the commanding general) and his staff believed that only three hundred Confederates were manning Fort Wagner. In reality, they numbered seventeen hundred.

Heavily gunned Fort Wagner was approachable only by a narrow stretch of beach. On the evening of July 18, as six hundred members of the 54th waited to open the assault, General Strong, on horseback, asked who would pick up the flag if the bearer fell.

"I will," replied Shaw. At the signal to attack, Shaw sent his horse back and led the charge on foot, sword in hand. When the enemy opened fire at two hundred yards, the flag bearer was instantly hit.

Seizing the flag, Shaw scrambled to the top of Fort Wagner's rampart and was shot just as he shouted, "Forward, Fifty-fourth!"

As the 54th's Sergeant William H. Carney, of New Bedford, reached the top of the fort, he picked up the flag from the fallen Shaw. Carney then fought his way down again, severely wounded, still holding the flag. "Boys, the old flag never touched the ground," said Carney (words soon famous all over the North) as he later staggered into the hospital tent, still bearing the "Stars and Stripes."

The national flag had tremendous importance in this war between Americans. The Union's "Stars and Stripes" and the Confederacy's "Southern Cross," which had replaced its earlier flag, "Stars and Bars," were symbols of two different countries and two different philosophies, representing the difference between freedom and slavery, as well as life and death. Carney's deed made him the first black recipient of the newly created Medal of Honor, the nation's highest military award for bravery.

"I escaped unhurt from amidst that perfect hail of shot and shell," wrote another survivor of Fort Wagner, Sergeant Major Lewis Douglass, to his fiancée:

> *This regiment has established its reputation as a fighting regiment, not a man flinched. . . . A shell would explode and clear a space of twenty feet, our men would close up again, but it was no use we had to retreat, which was a very dangerous undertaking. How I got out of that fight alive I cannot tell. . . . Remember if I die I die in a good cause. I wish we had a hundred thousand colored troops we would put an end to this war.*

One hundred and fifty members of the 54th had been killed or wounded before they even reached the rampart. The regiment suffered 50 percent casualties. Five out of the brigade's six commanders, including Colonel Shaw and General Strong, were killed or wounded. All told, the Union suffered 1,515 casualties; the Confederacy, 181.

The slain white officers of the 54th received a decent burial from the Confederates—except for Shaw, whose body was stripped and dumped into an unmarked mass grave with the slain black soldiers. After the battle, the Union commander sent a flag of truce requesting Shaw's body, as was customary with high-ranking officers. It was refused. "He is buried with his niggers" was the Confederate general Johnson Hagood's reply, according to the northern press. Although at least one Union witness denied that these were the actual words, they produced great bitterness throughout the North.

The Union soldiers captured at Fort Wagner went on to face another kind of battleground—the CSA's "hospital."

By modern lights, all Civil War hospital conditions, especially for prisoners, ranged from primitive to horrific. In his description of 1860's medical conditions in *Photographic History of the Civil War,* Major Edward L. Munson, a Union Army doctor, wrote: "Nothing in the way of antiseptics was provided . . . the cleanliness of wounds, except in respect to the gross forms of foreign matter, was regarded as of little or no importance." There was sometimes chloroform, or a little crude opium, but "several hundred major operations were reported during the war in which no anesthetic was employed." The South had a shortage of medical books and instruments, and no skilled instrument makers: surgical tools resembled hacksaws.

Sergeant Robert Simmons, a twenty-six-year-old native of Bermuda, was among the twenty-nine members of the 54th who were captured and taken to Charleston's "Yankee" hospital. Simmons's arm was amputated and he died in prison a month later.

On July 24, in a prisoner exchange in Charleston Harbor, wounded white Union soldiers complained of "neglected" wounds, "unskillful" surgeons, and "unnecessary" amputations. Black prisoners, said to have received treatment last, were not released at the time.

In mid-summer 1863, Lincoln issued his "eye for an eye" warning: for every white or black Union prisoner killed, a Confederate prisoner of war would be shot. For every black person enslaved, a rebel prisoner would be sentenced to life at hard labor.

Despite Lincoln's "eye for an eye" proclamation, the early months of 1864 saw atrocities committed against black soldiers.

In March, when Union troops defeated a numerically superior Confederate force under General Nathan Bedford Forrest at Fort Anderson, Kentucky, the humiliated Forrest sought revenge—something he got a few months later at Fort Pillow, near Memphis, Tennessee.

In the spring of 1864, Fort Pillow was manned by a force of less than six hundred black and white troops. On April 12, 1864, the fort was surrounded and stormed by fifteen hundred men of the Confederate cavalry under the command of General Forrest. Two hundred thirty-one Union soldiers, most of them black, were killed. A hundred were seriously wounded. One hundred sixty-eight whites and fifty-eight blacks were captured.

Southern accounts insisted that the Union soldiers were killed fighting for the fort, whereas northern reports maintained that the soldiers were massacred—along with black women and children inside the fort—after they had surrendered.

The Mississippi "was dyed with the blood of the slaughtered for 200 yards," wrote General Forrest in his report on Fort Pillow. He also stated that "these facts will demonstrate to the Northern people that negro soldiers cannot cope with Southerners." (After the war, Forrest became the leader of the Ku Klux Klan, a white supremacist and terrorist organization. Today, this anti-black, anti-Jewish, and anti-Catholic organization has chapters around the U.S.)

Six days after Fort Pillow, 1st Kansas soldiers were outnumbered by Confederates at Poison Spring, Arkansas. Southern troops fired on trapped and wounded blacks as Union forces retreated. Of the 438 members of the 1st Kansas, 182 were killed or missing. In the wake of the massacre, black troops east of the Mississippi went into battle shouting, "Remember Fort Pillow!"—as black troops in the West cried, "Remember Poison Spring!"

Most of 1864 was devoted to the siege and capture of the capital of the Confederacy, Richmond, Virginia, with black troops giving their all along the way. More than a dozen received Medals of Honor, with many more receiving commendations and high praise for their valor at Petersburg, Richmond's transportation center; at New Market Heights, south of Richmond; at nearby Fort Gilmer; and at Fort Fisher, in the harbor of Wilmington, North Carolina. Fort Fisher, conquered in mid-January 1865, had been the Confederacy's General Robert E. Lee's most important supply depot and last gateway to the outside world. A month after the surrender of Fort Fisher, Charleston fell. The first Union troops to enter the city were the 54th and 55th Massachusetts.

Richmond finally fell on April 2, 1865. Then, on April 9, 1865, General Lee surrendered to General Grant at Appomattox. For all intents and purposes, the war was over; the Confederacy, dead. On April 15, President Lincoln, by then in his second term, was dead, too. Furious that a Union victory would mean "nigger citizenship," the actor John Wilkes Booth had vowed to "put him through." On the night of April 14, as the president watched a play at Washington, D.C.'s Ford's Theatre, Booth shot him in the head. A few days later, black troops of the 22nd USCT led Lincoln's funeral procession down Pennsylvania Avenue. Two days later they joined in the hunt for John Wilkes Booth.

The last battle of the Civil War was a Confederate victory at Palmito Ranch, Texas, on May 12. The last Union soldier to be killed by a rebel bullet was black: Sergeant Bill Redman, of the 62nd USCT.

By the end of the war there were a little over 186,000 black enlisted men in the Union Army and a little over 7,100 black officers—mostly chaplains, surgeons, and battlefield commissions of 1865. There were some 30,000 black sailors in the Union Navy—and no black Navy officers. In the last twenty-three months of war, black soldiers and sailors had participated in 449 engagements, 39 of which were major battles. Roughly 68,000 died: about 2,700 in combat and the rest from wounds and disease. At 14 percent of the population, blacks counted for about 20 percent of the total Union casualties.

Despite the sacrifice and loss, much had been won. Most important for anti-slavery Americans was the Thirteenth

Amendment to the U.S. Constitution. Proposed in January 1865 and ratified the following December, the Thirteenth Amendment abolished slavery throughout America—"except as a punishment for crime," for which a person has been convicted.

In the Revolution, blacks had fought for the creation of a new country. With the Civil War, they finally won the right to live as free people in that country and to bear arms in its defense. The future looked bright for black soldiers.

BUFFALO SOLDIERS I

Perhaps no incidents in American history present a greater number of brilliant achievements, more thrilling experiences, more daring deeds, dramatic episodes, and bloody tragedies than those adventures which attended the pioneers of the Western plains . . . which characterized the conquests, development, and entire life of the United States Army in the far West, in its attempt to subdue the wild, hostile and savage Indian, for the purpose of advancing the civilization of the Western World. The great success of the Negro soldiery in this respect sufficiently vindicates their worth as efficient defenders of the country's flag and honor.

—Herschel V. Cashin, in *Under Fire with the Tenth U.S. Cavalry* (1899)

Exploring and charting the wilderness; building thousands of miles of roads and telegraph lines; escorting stagecoaches, wagon trains, railroad crews, and surveying parties; protecting homesteaders, ranchers, and the U.S. mail from outlaws—these were among the duties of the "New Army," established by Congress in July 1866 as part of the U.S. government's determination to "win the West." Soldiers in this New Army would fight the newest sectional war—between East and West instead of North and South—going up against armies of the Sioux, Apache, Kiowa, Comanche, and Cheyenne. For the U.S. government, subduing Native Americans—either by relocation or warfare—was critical to winning the West.

The newest thing about the New Army was that one in five of its men was black. These men would serve in two new cavalry regiments—the 9th and 10th—and two new infantry regiments—the 24th and the 25th. The New Army, like the old, mandated complete segregation for black soldiers, who would stay longer on the frontier, deserting less and reenlisting more than their white counterparts did.

Black troops were originally sent to isolated outposts such as Fort Leavenworth (Kansas), Fort Rice (present-day North Dakota), Fort Robinson (Nebraska), Fort Duchesne (present-day Utah), and Fort Washakie (present-day Wyoming)—all far away from white populations. As Native Americans were subdued and white settlements grew up on the plains, black units were generally concentrated in Texas and Arizona. Frontier race relations depended on the black–white–Native American ratio: where the Native American population was large, blacks might be treated fairly well.

Despite the isolation, the danger, and the inferior horses, equipment, and food, the Army had great appeal for many blacks: Army pay of $13 per month was far better than most black men could hope to earn as civilians. In five years without leave, many made the best of it, saving money and learning to read and write. They also perfected their skills: black cavalry troopers would be put in charge of West Point riding instruction, and black military marksmanship became famous. Black soldiers were eventually considered among the New Army's best. Eighteen Medals of Honor out of four hundred sixteen awarded between 1866 and 1891 went to black troopers. Many of their white officers were similarly rewarded, which often indicated the quality of the troops.

In 1867, when eight hundred Cheyenne were defeated by ninety troopers of the 10th Cavalry in a two-day battle near Fort Leavenworth, Kansas—with a loss of only three cavalrymen— black scalps became highly prized. One Cheyenne was said to have cut up a buffalo hide to make and sell black "scalps." Comparing them to an animal they considered sacred, the

Cheyenne called 10th Cavalry troopers Buffalo Soldiers. The term came to apply to all black western units. It was said that Native Americans later refrained from scalping blacks and, in fact, did not relish fighting them.

The "Buffalo Soldiers" of the 10th Cavalry first assembled at Fort Leavenworth, Kansas, near the Nebraska and Iowa borders, in the spring of 1867, under Colonel Benjamin Grierson, a famous Union Army cavalry officer. Leavenworth was an unrelenting war zone for the 10th—against racist whites as well as Native Americans. Upon the 10th's arrival at Leavenworth, the fort commander, Colonel William Hoffman, assigned the regiment to a bog. Then, calling their uniforms filthy, Hoffman ordered them not to come within fifteen yards of whites, even on the parade grounds.

The same year that the 10th arrived at Leavenworth, the Indian Peace Commission, formed by Congress, created a system of reservations for Native Americans. They hoped the reservation system would put an end to Plains warfare and keep Native Americans as far away as possible from settlers and railroads. Treaties with the Cheyenne and Arapahoe removed them to a 4-million-acre reservation in what is today Oklahoma, between the Washita and Red Rivers. A similar reservation tract of 3 million acres, immediately to the south of the Cheyenne-Arapahoe, went to the Comanche, Kiowa, and Kiowa-Apaches. The Native Americans retained the right to hunt buffalo anywhere south of the Arkansas River, and the U.S. government provided food and clothing. The reservation system would prove anything but successful, and broken treaties—by white civilians as well as by soldiers—came to symbolize the white man's "forked tongue," and very often met with revenge attacks by Native Americans. And the cycle of violence continued.

In November 1868, General George Armstrong Custer led a surprise attack on the Washita River encampment of Cheyenne Chief Black Kettle, indiscriminately killing men, women, children, dogs, and horses. The same pattern of warfare raged on the Texas border with Kiowas and Comanches, whom the 10th Cavalry would also fight in Oklahoma, Texas, New Mexico, and Arizona.

West Texas was known as the Soldier's Paradise, possibly because there was so much to shoot at. "Beautiful rivers, grass and grassy plains, teemed with game," wrote Captain William G. Muller in *The 24th Infantry Past and Present.* "The buffalo overran the plains in the autumn; immense herds of antelope, thousands of deer, wild turkeys, quail, duck and geese were everywhere—not to speak of cattle run wild, by the thousands, free to anyone."

In 1873, seven companies of the 10th Cavalry were sent to this "paradise." Stationed at several forts, including Forts Richardson and Concho, they shared Indian-fighting duties with the 9th Cavalry and the 24th and 25th Infantries, all based at Fort McKavett.

About 180 miles from San Antonio, on the edge of the great Staked Plain of west Texas and New Mexico, McKavett was the most remote outpost of the frontier. In the spring of 1875, two companies of the 24th Infantry, one company of the 25th, nine 10th Cavalry troopers, and several Native American scouts left the fort for a seven-month expedition to explore the plains. They marched, William Muller recalled, thirty miles a day "over a country like an ocean of waving grass," traveling with a pack train of about seven hundred mules, sixty-five six-mule wagons, and a herd of cattle, as buffalo lumbered out of the way and antelope turned to gaze "in wonder." They trekked through the Texas Serengeti from early May through Christmas Eve, suffering much hardship. "During the last lap . . . the officers . . . having lost all hope, had gotten together and written messages to be taken home by any who might survive."

Finally reaching "civilization" at New Mexico's Pecos River, the infantry was sent out in detachments to raid Native American villages. Some five hundred to a thousand ponies were captured, with "a lot of squaws, who were taken to Fort Duncan, but subsequently escaped." The expedition was mapped by a 10th Cavalry second lieutenant.

In July 1875, six companies of the 10th Cavalry, two companies of the 24th Infantry, and one company of the 25th were part of Lieutenant Colonel William R. Shafter's famous expedition to explore even further the Staked Plain. According to congressional orders, the purpose of the expedition was to "show in detail the resources of the country, looking to its adaptability for cultivation and stock-raising." They were also to deal with Comanches resisting white rule. Soon after the expedition, cattlemen and homesteaders started to migrate to the area.

The Indian Wars coincided with the era of Radical Reconstruction, during which time the government sponsored and supported initiatives for black political and economic progress.

Back in 1865, President Andrew Johnson had sent General Carl Schurz to investigate southern conditions. Schurz's report was hair-raising:

Dead bodies of murdered Negroes were found on and near the highways and by-ways. Gruesome reports came from the hospitals—reports of colored men and women whose ears had been cut off, whose skulls had been broken by blows, whose bodies had been slashed by knives or lacerated with scourges. A number of such cases, I had occasion to examine myself. A . . . reign of terror prevailed in many parts of the South.

President Johnson, no friend to blacks, was displeased by Schurz's report. It gave radical Republicans—those who supported justice for black people—the upper hand. The old abolitionists Senator Charles Sumner of Massachusetts and Representative Thaddeus Stevens of Pennsylvania created a congressional committee, which radically "reconstructed" the South, dividing the former Confederacy into five military districts occupied by federal troops and controlled by generals.

Reconstruction milestones included the Civil Rights Act of 1866 and in 1868, the Fourteenth Amendment, which declared "all persons born or naturalized in the United States" citizens of the United States. The amendment also stated that "no State shall make or enforce any law which shall abridge the privileges or immunities of citizens of the United States; nor shall any State deprive any person of life, liberty, or property, without due process of law; nor deny to any person within its jurisdiction the equal protection of the laws." Another milestone, the Fifteenth Amendment, was ratified in February 1870 and gave black men the right to the national vote. (Women would not receive it until 1920.) The overwhelming majority of blacks would vote Republican. "The Republican Party is the ship," said Frederick Douglass, "all else is the sea."

During Reconstruction a number of blacks held government posts. Among them was Douglass, whose jobs included the recorder of deeds and the U.S. marshal for Washington, D.C. Blacks also held political office. Two former officers of the 1st Louisiana Native Guards became lieutenant governors of Louisiana: Oscar J. Dunn in 1868, and, in 1872, Cesar C. Antoine. There would be twenty-two blacks in Congress, including three senators (two of whom were veterans).

The Civil Rights Bill of 1875, which banned discrimination in public facilities, such as hospitals, cemeteries, theaters, restaurants, boats, and trains, was another positive for blacks. (The bill originally contained a school-desegregation clause, which was deleted when the bill passed. Public-school desegregation would not become law until 1954.)

Black advancement in the military became a possibility during Reconstruction when the War Department insisted on the creation of a small group of black Army staff-officers—whether the United States Military Academy liked it or not.

After the Revolution, George Washington, among others, had proposed the idea of an official military academy. In 1802, Congress established the United States Military Academy at West Point, above the Hudson River Palisades, about fifty miles north of New York City. Civil War generals Robert E. Lee and Ulysses S. Grant were among the famous graduates of this academy, commonly referred to as West Point.

From 1870 to 1898, twenty-three blacks were appointed to West Point. Twelve actually attended, six stayed longer than one semester, and only three graduated. None were welcomed. In July

1870, President Grant's own cadet son swore to his father that "no . . . nigger will ever graduate from West Point."

James Smith, a native of South Carolina admitted to West Point in 1870, was well prepared academically and determined to graduate. Smith had arrived with (and roomed with) another black plebe, Michael Howard, of Mississippi. The two did not have one peaceful day.

"We could not meet a cadet anywhere without having the most opprobrious epithets applied to us." Smith and Howard complained once or twice, but to no avail. They then decided to ignore the taunts—until a slops pail was dumped over them while they slept, and then a white cadet struck Howard in the face for being "in the way." The slops dumper remained undiscovered, and the cadet who hit Howard received a slap on the wrist. (Michael Howard failed his first exams and left.)

When Smith was in his last year, a white man who visited West Point found that when it came to Smith, "a system of terrorism reigned supreme." This man reported that Smith spoke "slowly," as if he had "lost the use of language." Smith was dismissed in June 1874, just before graduation, for failing a philosophy course. He died from tuberculosis two years later.

By the time Smith left West Point, four other black men had entered. Three were discharged within a year of their arrival for "deficiencies" in one or more subjects. The fourth was the native of Thomasville, Georgia, Henry Ossian Flipper, who had been appointed to the Academy from Atlanta University in 1873.

Flipper was the sixth black cadet to enter West Point. He had arrived a semi-celebrity, having refused $5,000 from a white man who wanted Flipper's place for his son. Year after year, Flipper's West Point career was tracked by the press.

Flipper found the white cadets friendly at first. The insults and ostracism started a month or so after he arrived. Flipper did not regularly fight back. He was disposed to overlook, to forgive and forget. "One must endure these little tortures—the sneer, the shrug of the shoulder, the epithet, the effort to avoid, to disdain, to ignore," Flipper wrote in his memoir *The Colored Cadet at West Point.* Flipper complained to authorities only on very rare occasions, as when a junior cadet sought to have him removed from his assigned seat in chapel.

As a plebe, Flipper had often heard himself spoken of as "the nigger," "the moke," or "the thing." In time, "openly, and when my presence was not known," he heard himself referred to as "Mr. Flipper." Flipper's approaching graduation became a news story. *The New York Times* did not believe that he would graduate. A black newspaper was sure that he would "eventually be slaughtered" one way or another. But Flipper made it: he became the first black person to do what President Grant's son had sworn no black would ever do. A photo of Flipper—handsome, confident, and splendidly uniformed—appeared in the class graduation album, but he was not in the group picture.

"When Mr. Flipper, the colored cadet, stepped forward and received the reward of four years of as hard work and unflinching courage as any young man can be called upon to go through," wrote *The New York Times* of June 15, 1877, "the crowd of spectators gave him a round of applause." *The New York Tribune* believed Flipper had "made matters easier" for future black cadets: "Twenty years hence, if not sooner, the young white gentlemen of West Point will read of the fastidiousness of their predecessors with incredulous wonder. Time and patience will settle everything."

After graduation, Flipper joined the 10th Cavalry. He had

refused an offer from the government of Liberia to become commander of its army in order to be the only black officer in the U.S. Army—and the only black officer of black troops. When Flipper joined the 10th Cavalry, he also gave up love: in January 1878, when the 10th was sent to Fort Sill, Oklahoma, his fiancée's family forbade the marriage because Indian Territory was too dangerous.

Flipper's duties were intense and varied. They included installing telegraph lines and supervising the building of the road from Fort Sill to Gainesville, Oklahoma. His engineering skills continued to impress the Army as well as his white fellow-officers. He designed a ditch to drain cesspools suspected of breeding malaria, which is still known as Flipper's Ditch. Flipper also served as a scout and a messenger for the 10th Cavalry's leader, Colonel Benjamin H. Grierson, in the famous 1880–1881 campaign against Victorio, leader of the Warm Springs Apaches, who was incensed by Indian Bureau insistence that all Apaches move to the dreaded San Carlos reservation in the Arizona desert. (General John Pope had written to General Philip Sheridan that no one could expect to survive at San Carlos.)

In August 1879, Victorio left the reservation for the mountains of northern Mexico, from where he sent out raiding parties. He was pursued by the U.S. and Mexican armies, the Texas Rangers, and civilian posses. His capture and killing, in October 1881, at Tres Castillos in northern Chihuahua broke the back of the Apache uprising. Two members of the 9th Cavalry, Sergeants George Jordan and Thomas Shaw, won Medals of Honor for their actions at Tres Castillos.

Flipper was eventually transferred to the desolate outpost of Fort Davis in Texas, where he served as quartermaster (the officer in charge of troop supplies) and acting commissary officer. At

Fort Davis, Flipper had to contend with three very hostile officers, one of whom was the explorer and camp commander
Colonel William R. Shafter.

In August 1881, Flipper was falsely accused of embezzlement
and subsequently arrested. In December, twenty-five-year-old
Flipper was found innocent of embezzlement, but guilty of "conduct unbecoming an officer and gentleman," which automatically
incurred a dishonorable discharge. Flipper's post-military career
included a highly successful mining and surveying career in the
Southwest and Mexico. Flipper died in Atlanta in 1940, having
petitioned Congress nine times to clear his name. Flipper's name
was finally cleared in 1976 thanks to the efforts of a white Georgia
schoolteacher named Ray McColl, who became obsessed with
Flipper's case. In 1977, West Point established the Henry O. Flipper
Memorial Award for "leadership, self-discipline and perseverance in
the face of unusual difficulties while a cadet." He was reburied with
military honors in 1978. In 1999, Flipper received an official presidential pardon from President William Jefferson Clinton.

Flipper's triumph at West Point did not in the short term make
"matters easier" for future black cadets, as *The New York Tribune* had
hoped—definitely not for Johnson Chestnut Whittaker, a former
slave from South Carolina. When Whittaker entered West Point in
1876, he roomed with Flipper. When Flipper graduated, eighteen-
year-old Whittaker became West Point's only black cadet.

Whittaker had no friends and no social life. His only solace
was daily Bible reading. On April 4, 1880, two months before
graduation, he received a scribbled note: "You will be fixed. Better
keep awake. A friend." Later that night, Whittaker was found

unconscious in his room—beaten, slashed, and tied to his bed. He reported that he had been beaten and cut during the night by three masked attackers, who burned pages of his Bible.

The commandant of cadets insisted that Whittaker had slashed and bound himself, because he was afraid of failing a philosophy course. Demanding a court of inquiry to clear his name, Whittaker became the subject of national attention and congressional debate. Public opinion was generally on his side. Whittaker's court-martial commenced in January 1881, and he was found guilty. The verdict was overturned that fall, but by then Whittaker was no longer at West Point: he had been dismissed for failing his philosophy course.

The U.S. Naval Academy in Annapolis, Maryland, (established 1845), commonly referred to by its place name, was even more successful than West Point at getting rid of would-be black officers. John Henry Conyers was the first black man admitted to Annapolis, in 1872, but he resigned within a year. Alonzo McClennan entered Annapolis in September 1873 and resigned in March 1874, after two faculty members promised to pay for his education anywhere else. McClennan entered medical school and became a successful physician. In September 1874, an officer had to brandish his sword to protect McClennan's successor, Henry E. Baker of Mississippi, from his fellow midshipmen. Baker was dismissed the following November, but he also landed on his feet, becoming a clerk in the U.S. Patent Office. Three more black candidates were appointed in the 1870s, but none actually entered. (There would not be another black midshipman at Annapolis until 1949, Wesley A. Brown.)

* * *

The beginning of the end of Reconstruction came in the deadlocked presidential election of 1876. The resulting compromise allowed Ohio Republican Rutherford B. Hayes to be President if he would agree to remove federal troops from the South. This meant that white supremacists would have freer rein to terrorize blacks and prevent them from exercising their civil rights, including voting. For example, in 1878 in Abbeville, South Carolina, three blacks voted as compared to 1,500 in 1874.

Tennessee, birthplace of the Ku Klux Klan, segregated its railroad cars in 1881 and invented the legal system known as Jim Crow, after "Jump Jim Crow," a minstrel song. Jim Crow laws swiftly followed in Florida, Mississippi, Texas, Louisiana, Alabama, Kentucky, Arkansas, Virginia, Maryland, and Oklahoma. In 1883, the U.S. Supreme Court declared the 1875 Civil Rights Bill unconstitutional on the grounds that the Fourteenth Amendment prohibited states but not individuals from discriminating. By the end of the nineteenth century, Jim Crow was very much in force around the nation, owing to the U.S. Supreme Court's 1896 ruling in the *Plessy v. Ferguson* case that segregation was constitutional.

Also by the end of the nineteenth century, the U.S. government had fulfilled its wish to control the West, with Buffalo Soldiers earning high marks in several of the last campaigns against Native Americans. In Arizona, the 10th Cavalry fought in the 1885–1886 campaign against the great Apache warrior Geronimo. Medals of Honor were awarded to black troopers in 1890 for bravery in the last Indian campaigns. Sergeant William McBryar, of the 10th Cavalry, was cited for actions against the Apaches in Arizona; and Corporal William O. Wilson, of the 9th Cavalry, was cited for the Sioux campaign.

"Many causes are ascribed for the outbreak among the various Indian tribes throughout Montana and the Dakotas in the winter of 1890–'91," wrote Colonel Philip Harvey, of the 25th Infantry, "but there can be little doubt that the condition of destitution . . . brought about by reduced rations and the dishonesty and mismanagement of minor government officials had a far reaching effect." One major effect was that Colonel Harvey's 25th Infantry and the 9th Cavalry joined the white 7th Cavalry to fight the last Indian war, on December 29, 1890, against near-starving and destitute Sioux encamped on the banks of a South Dakota creek called Wounded Knee.

By 1890, two more black men had graduated from West Point. The first was the son of former slaves, John H. Alexander. This native of Arkansas was a freshman at Oberlin College when he received his appointment in 1882. After graduation, Alexander joined the 9th Cavalry, serving in Nebraska, Wyoming, and Utah. In 1894 he became professor of military science and tactics at Wilberforce University in Ohio. Alexander died the same year, at thirty, of a heart attack.

The next black man to enter West Point was Charles Young, born in Kentucky to former slaves (and whose father had served in the Union Army). Young spent five years at West Point, repeating a year because he failed a math course. He seems to have made friends with other cadets, and was possibly only "semi-silenced." In 1889, he became the third black man to graduate from West Point (and with the entrenchment of Jim Crow, not until 1936 would there be another). Young went on to join the 9th Cavalry, and eventually became professor of military science and tactics at Wilberforce. Charles Young's military career would be continually stifled during and after the Spanish-American War.

BUFFALO SOLDIERS II

At San Juan Hill three companies of the Twenty-fourth Infantry . . . lost every one of their officers before the fighting was over. . . . It is said that the Twenty-fourth bore the brunt of the battles around Santiago, the Spaniards directing their main attack upon them on the theory that the Negroes would not stand the punishment. Yet whole companies remained steady without a single officer.

—The Springfield, Illinois, *Republican*

On February 15, 1898, 266 American sailors, of whom 22 were black, were killed when the battleship *Maine* blew up in the harbor of Havana, Cuba, then controlled by Spain. American popular opinion, encouraged by the press, blamed a Spanish bomb. (Later study indicated that the real cause was probably an accidental shipboard explosion.)

At the time of the explosion, the majority of Americans wanted revenge. They wanted war. Most black Americans supported a war with Spain. Cuba was considered a "colored" country, and the Cuban rebel leader General Antonio Maceo, the African-Indian-Spanish architect of *Cuba libre* (Free Cuba) murdered by the Spanish in 1896, became a martyr to black Americans. The U.S. government's willingness to go to war, however, was clearly more about sugar, tobacco, and bananas than about Cuba's liberation from Spain. The *Maine* had been sent to Havana harbor to keep an eye on American interests in Cuba during the 1895 U.S.-supported Cuban revolution.

In early March, Congress passed the Fifty Million Dollar Bill, which granted President William McKinley that amount of money to ready the armed forces for war. In April, America demanded that Spain grant Cuba its independence. When Spain refused, on April 25, America declared war on Spain. "Remember the *Maine*, to hell with Spain!" was the catchy battle cry.

On May 1, John Jordan, a black gunner's mate, led the crew that fired the first American shots of the war—not in Cuba, but from Commodore George Dewey's flagship in Manila Bay, in the Philippines, also controlled by Spain. At battle's end, the Spanish fleet had been obliterated. With the help of anti-Spanish insurgents, American victory in the Philippines was assured. But before America took total control of the Philippines came the battles in Cuba. U.S. forces landed in the Cuban town of Daiquirí on June 22, 1898.

In March 1898, the 25th Infantry became the first American troops ordered to Tampa, Florida, for deployment to Cuba, some ninety miles away.

All along the way, cities and towns offered noisy demonstrations of gratitude to the men in dark blue shirts, khaki breeches, and cowboy hats. When the 25th Infantry troop train reached St. Paul, Minnesota, the engine was decorated with flags, and crowds gathered at the station. Goodwill toward black soldiers stopped at the Mason-Dixon Line. In the South, the reception was chilly, "even though these brave men were rushing to the front in the very face of grim death to defend the flag and preserve the country's honor and dignity," wrote Herschel V. Cashin in *Under Fire with the Tenth U.S. Cavalry*. Cashin reached Tampa in May with the 24th Infantry.

The Buffalo Soldiers weren't the only black soldiers being

readied for war. Shortly after war was declared, the War Department authorized four new regiments of black troops: the 7th through 10th U.S. Volunteer Infantries, with mostly white officers. From one of these new regiments came the man who would become America's first black general: Lieutenant Benjamin O. Davis, at Fort Thomas, Kentucky, where his regiment, the 8th Volunteers, trained under old Buffalo Soldiers.

Davis, born and raised in Washington, D.C., had wanted to be a cavalry officer ever since one of the parents at his primary school, an ex–Civil War officer, organized a school drill group. Young Davis's military motivation was further strengthened in 1893 by the sight of the 9th Cavalry marching in the inaugural parade of President Grover Cleveland. Later, at his high school (the future Dunbar High School), Davis became captain of the Cadet Corps. He had volunteered as soon as America declared war on Spain.

Davis never saw battle in Cuba and neither did Charles Young. At the onset of war, thirty-four-year-old First Lieutenant Charles Young, 9th Cavalry, West Point class of 1889, was the only black officer in the regular Army qualified to lead troops in combat. From his post as military instructor at Wilberforce University, Young wrote to the War Department asking to rejoin his regiment when it was called to active service. The 9th Cavalry went to Cuba, but Young did not. Instead, he became a major (wartime rank) in the 9th Ohio U.S. Volunteers, serving in Virginia, Pennsylvania, and South Carolina. West Point or not, black officers would not lead black troops in battle.

Like the Civil War, the Spanish-American War was an enormous media event, covered in newspapers, magazines, and even motion pictures. What was described as "an army of correspondents and artists" arrived along with the Army and Navy. Photography was still in its relative infancy. Action shots were impossible, so sketch artists and painters were called upon to provide action stills. The outfit that claimed the lion's share of public attention was the 1st Volunteer Cavalry, better known as the Rough Riders: Colonel Theodore Roosevelt's semi-private army of Texas cowboys and eastern Ivy Leaguers. But Roosevelt's Rough Riders owed much of their glory, as well as their lives, to the Buffalo Soldiers who came to their rescue in three important battles.

The initial bonding of white volunteers and black professional soldiers involved a Rough Rider rescue of Buffalo Soldiers during the Daiquirí landings. When a boat carrying men of the 10th Cavalry capsized, a Rough Rider captain and several sailors dived into the sea to help.

Rough Riders and Buffalo Soldiers bonded again on the fast-paced march from Daiquirí to Siboney, when men tossed away clothing, packs, and blankets because of the intense heat. On June 24, two days after landing, they met the enemy at Las Guásimas: together, fewer than a thousand Rough Riders and 10th Cavalry troopers fought two thousand Spanish soldiers and destroyed the outpost.

At Las Guásimas it was the Rough Riders who were in trouble. Using old Indian-fighting techniques, 10th Cavalry troopers saved a trapped Rough Rider squadron. *The Washington Post* correspondent at the battle scene expressed his personal gratitude:

> *If it had not been for the Negro cavalry, the Rough Riders would have been exterminated. I am not a Negro lover. My*

71

father fought with Mosby's Rangers [a freelance unit that fought for the Confederacy] and I was born in the South, but the Negroes saved that fight, and the day will come when General Shafter will give them credit for their bravery.

The rotund, walrus-mustached General William R. Shafter, ex-tormentor of Lieutenant Flipper, was commander of the American forces.

Another man who lived to tell of Las Guásimas was a veteran of the last Apache campaign, the 10th Cavalry's Sergeant Horace W. Bivens, the thirty-six-year-old Virginian who was in charge of a battery of Hotchkiss guns. "The First and Tenth . . . regiments . . . charged up the hill in front," Bivens recalled in *Under Fire with the Tenth U.S. Cavalry*, "driving the enemy from their position, but not until we had sustained a severe loss in both killed and wounded. . . . The conduct of the troops, both white and colored . . . was most gallant and soldierly."

A few days after Las Guásimas, more black soldiers proved themselves "most gallant and soldierly" in San Juan Heights, outside of Santiago de Cuba, where the Spanish forces had retreated after the fight at Las Guásimas. They had dug in at two hilltop spots: the village of El Caney and San Juan Hill.

On July 1, General Shafter gave the order for the American forces to attack. The first assault was upon El Caney—known as Hell Caney. William Glackens's painting *The Twelfth and Twenty-fifth Infantry Taking the Blockhouse at El Caney* has the energy and drama of an action photograph. The 25th Infantry captured the Spanish flag, but white troops of the 12th Infantry jumped their claim.

In the midst of the battle, when white troops from New York

were reluctant to fight, the 24th, in the rear of and supporting the white 13th Infantry, asked to take the lead. "The Thirteenth Infantry needed no further invitation but immediately stepped to the left of the road," wrote Herschel V. Cashin. As the 24th passed by the 13th, they met General J. Ford Kent at a fork in the road, "with tears running down his cheeks, begging, admonishing, persuading and entreating the Seventy-first New York Volunteers (white), 'for the love of country, liberty, honor and dignity . . . to stand up like men and fight, and go to the front.' But all in vain, they fled like sheep from the presence of wolves."

Soon after they passed the 71st, the 24th "rushed like madmen" into the river, wrote Cashin, crossing with water up to their necks. Once on land, they broke through wire fences and "rushed wildly across the open field, attracting the attention of the entire Spanish line, and drawing their concentrated fire." When the hill was taken, the commanding general sent congratulations to the 24th, ordering "that they be not required to fire another gun that day." The regiment had suffered major losses. Companies numbering one hundred men now reported as few as twenty—or fewer.

Public attention focused on the courage of the black regiments in both the Battle of El Caney and the Battle of San Juan Hill. Of the 9th's performance at San Juan Hill, *The New York Sun* reported the following:

> *The soldiers leaped forward, charging and shooting across the field . . . to the river. . . . Across the stream they went, and up the other side, the Spaniards pouring shot into them at a lively rate. They could no more stop the advance, however, than they could have stopped an avalanche.*

Rough Rider Frank Knox (a future secretary of the Navy) had nothing but praise for the men of the 10th with whom he fought "shoulder to shoulder" when he was separated from his unit. "In justice to the colored race," said Knox, "I must say that I never saw braver men anywhere. Some of these who rushed up the hill will live in my memory forever."

The 10th Cavalry lost 20 percent of its men and half its officers at San Juan Hill. Five 10th Cavalry troopers won Medals of Honor: Privates Dennis Bell, Fritz Lee, William H. Thompkins, and George Wanton, and Sergeant Major Edward L. Baker.

There was a time when the Rough Riders' commander, Theodore Roosevelt, would praise the Buffalo Soldiers and say, "I don't think that any Rough Rider will ever forget the tie that binds us to the 9th and 10th Cavalry." However, shortly after San Juan Hill, Roosevelt betrayed the Buffalo Soldiers. For one, he claimed that all black accomplishment was the result of white leadership. Worse, he invented a falsehood of encountering black troops drifting away from the battlefield and forcing them at gunpoint to return. The account was challenged in the black press by the 10th Cavalry's Sergeant Presley Holliday, who reported that Roosevelt had actually stopped four men on their way to the supply point to pick up ammunition. Roosevelt capitalized on his Rough Rider experience to become governor of New York in 1899 and vice president under McKinley in 1900, becoming president in 1901 following McKinley's assassination.

On July 16, 1898, Spanish forces under General Toral surrendered Santiago de Cuba. A little over a week later, U.S. and Spanish forces clashed in another Spanish colony: Puerto Rico. By August

11, U.S. forces had prevailed. Puerto Rico was not, however, the last battleground. The Spanish-American War ended where it began: in the Philippines, with Spanish forces surrendering Manila on August 14 after a light American assault. On December 10, 1898, the Treaty of Paris was signed, with Spain granting Cuba independence and ceding to America Puerto Rico, Guam, and, for $20 million, the Philippines.

After the war, all black volunteer regiments were disbanded and black officers of volunteer regiments were decommissioned. Blacks could still become noncommissioned officers (NCOs), but all black officers returned to the regular Army as enlisted men. Fewer than ten blacks would become commissioned officers in the regular Army between 1899 and 1948.

Benjamin O. Davis became one of those few black officers in 1901. After his regiment was disbanded in 1899, Davis applied for an Army commission but was rejected. He decided to enlist in the regular Army for two years and then take the officers exam. Sent to the 9th Cavalry at Fort Duchesne, Utah, Davis joined Troop I, known as Old Soldiers Home for its many veterans of the Indian Wars. When Charles Young returned to Fort Duchesne in 1900 from duty at Wilberforce, he coached Davis in mathematics for the coming exam. In 1901, Davis and John E. Green were the only blacks to receive commissions—they were among the last for a very long time. Both men's sons, however, would graduate from West Point and lead men in war.

Not long after the Treaty of Paris, the U.S. military was back in battle for absolute control of the Philippines. The same insurgents who had helped drive the Spanish out rose up against U.S. control.

The *"Insurrectos"* and their leader, General Emilio Aguinaldo, known as Aquino, set up a government on the island of Luzon and prepared to attack U.S. forces based in Manila. When the fighting broke out in early February 1899, the American force of twelve thousand was faced with the possibility of imminent extermination at the hands of some forty thousand insurgents. Among the desperately needed volunteer regiments authorized by the emergency act of March 2, 1899, were two new black regiments: the 48th and 49th Volunteer Infantries. They followed Buffalo Soldiers across the Pacific.

The 24th and 25th Infantries left for the Philippines from San Francisco in late June 1899. Like other U.S. troops, they found the jungle, forest, and mountain terrain even more difficult than Cuba's as well as an enemy far more dangerous because he was everywhere and hidden. They also faced heat, rain, fever, and leeches. They wore uniforms left over from Cuba. Often there was no food, water, or medicine.

Black America had a genuine hero in Captain Charles Young during the Philippine insurrection. In April 1901, he went to the Philippines, leading troops against rebels in the jungles of Samar, Blanca Aurora, Durago, Tobacco, and Rosano for eighteen months—and earning the nickname Follow Me!

Filipino resistance collapsed in central Luzon in the spring of 1901, when Aquino was captured and subsequently accepted "the sovereignty of the United States throughout the entire archipelago." Approximately seventy thousand U.S. troops had fought to crush the Filipino independence movement.

Some U.S. troops began returning home in the summer of

1902. Others, including the 24th Infantry, remained in the Philippines as troubles continued, especially among Muslims in the southern islands. In August 1906, when soldiers of the 24th and members of the new Philippine constabulary killed more than fifty insurgents on Leyte, significant opposition was destroyed.

With 1906 came the birth of the modern segregated Navy. When Japan defeated Russia in 1905, America worried about the security of the Philippines. In 1907 the "Great White Fleet," a brand-new American battle fleet, all painted white, sailed around the world: the aim was to impress Japan with the power of the Caucasian race. The Great White Fleet represented the new, all-white Navy—the first Navy in American history without black sailors. Blacks could be only stewards and messmen. It was also in 1906 that black soldiers were at the center of a major battle at home.

In the summer of 1906, when 170 men of the 25th Infantry's 1st Battalion were sent to Fort Brown, in Brownsville, Texas, to train with the Texas National Guard, the Army's commanding general in Texas had warned that "Citizens of Brownsville entertain race hatred to an extreme degree." The men of the 25th were welcomed to Brownsville by silent, hostile citizens and by signs barring blacks from stores and parks.

When shots were fired near Fort Brown on the night of August 13, the 25th, assuming a white attack, broke open locked rifle racks, and the bugler roused the camp. Meanwhile, one civilian was dead and several others were wounded.

Eight out of twenty-two self-proclaimed eyewitnesses, all

local men, said that the late-night gunmen were black soldiers. Some reported seeing men with revolvers, weapons not used by the 25th. Morning revealed cartridges and clips from Army Springfield rifles lying in the street.

Texans called it the Brownsville Raid and portrayed the men of the 25th as murderous savages. To a man, the 25th denied knowledge of the shooting. They were accused of shielding the guilty and ordered by the War Department to name the gunmen or face summary dismissal.

There were two Brownsville investigations. Although the final report stated that the "extreme penalty" would fall on "a number of men who have no direct knowledge of the identity" of the shooters, President Theodore Roosevelt accepted the recommendation for dismissal. He added later that some members of the 25th were clearly "bloody butchers" who "ought to be hung." One hundred sixty-seven soldiers of the 1st Battalion (three were on leave) were dishonorably discharged without a public hearing. They were forever barred from serving the government as either soldiers or civilians. (The men were exonerated following a 1972 reinvestigation. By then, Dorsie W. Willis was the only surviving member of the 25th troopers who had been at Brownsville. Along with his honorable discharge, Willis was granted $25,000 and medical treatment at a Veterans Administration hospital.)

In the wake of Brownsville, blacks turned away from Theodore Roosevelt and the Republican Party. The Brownsville incident was fuel to racist fire. A congressional bill was introduced calling for the removal of all blacks from the Army by mid-1907. The bill did not pass, and so blacks continued to serve in the military. The 25th Infantry, for example, fought hostile Moro tribesmen in the Philippines in 1907 and 1908. In the summer of 1910, they fought devastating forest fires in the Pacific Northwest. But they would spend 1913 to 1918 in Hawaii, sitting out World War I, like all Buffalo Soldiers.

WORLD WAR I

> *I shall never forget those fields covered with their silent motionless figures clad in the khaki of the United States, the horizon blue of France and the field gray of the Germans. Many of those bodies lay, for ten days in the hot sun before the pioneers, sappers and bombers, etc., came along to bury them, and to eat and sleep in such a place was not at all pleasant.*
>
> —Sergeant Clinton Peterson, of the 369th regiment, in a 1919 article for New York's *Putnam County Courier*

On June 28, 1914, a Serbian nationalist in Sarajevo assassinated Archduke Franz Ferdinand, heir to the Austro-Hungarian throne. A month later, Austria declared war on Serbia. Other nations quickly took sides, and what was once called the Great War and the World War had begun.

Russia supported Serbia, Germany supported Austria, France supported Russia, and Britain supported France. In August, Germany declared war on Russia and France and invaded neutral Belgium in order to attack France. Britain then declared war on Germany. "The Allies," the French-British contingent, eventually included Montenegro and Italy. The "Central Powers," the German-Austrian contingent, eventually included Bulgaria and Turkey. America remained officially neutral until April 2, 1917, when President Woodrow Wilson, stating that "the world must be made safe for democracy," asked Congress to declare war on Germany. In June, the first American soldiers arrived in Saint-Nazaire, France, the principal port of U.S. debarkation.

"The spectacle of these magnificent youths from overseas . . .

radiating strength and health," wrote an aide to Marshal Philippe Pétain, symbolized "life coming in floods to reanimate the dying body of France." Half of the "magnificent youths" barely spoke English (over 6 million new immigrants had arrived in America between 1907 and 1917) and most were illiterate. Americans were seen as ill-trained, ill-mannered, and sloppily uniformed—but great fighters.

Trench warfare was one of many new horrors these great fighters faced. Soldiers on both sides stood in muddy, rat-infested, and often corpse-filled trenches (suffering "trench feet" and "trench fever") until it was time to go "over the top." Wounds of a new kind were inflicted by weapons like *Minnenwerfer* (mortar filled with scrap metal), flamethrowers, machine guns, and fearsome German 150mm explosive shells.

A sense of doom was shared by all nationalities at the front. Fought mostly in the ore-rich territory of Belgium and northern France, the war was a no-man's-land of barbed wire and trenches. By the end of four years of war, some nine to twelve million people on both sides would be dead.

When America declared war on Germany, blacks were refused at many recruiting stations. But the new Selective Service Act of May 1917 mandated the enlistment of all able-bodied men aged twenty-one to thirty-one. Like the foreign-born, blacks would be overdrafted. By July 5, 1917, more than 700,000 blacks were registered; less than 10 percent of the U.S. population, they made up 13 percent of all U.S. draftees.

Of the roughly 368,000 black draftees who ultimately served, the vast majority were assigned to labor, supply, and service units. Only 11 percent of all black military forces would see combat. These combat troops would serve in two new black divisions: the

92nd, which would serve under the American flag; and the 93rd, which would serve with French forces.

At the onset of the war, there were approximately ten thousand blacks in the regular Army, all members of the four Buffalo Soldier regiments. There were also ten thousand black National Guardsmen. Some ten thousand blacks were in the Navy, all members of the noncombat mess and stewards' branches (a significant number of whom would die in combat when their ships were torpedoed). There were no blacks in the Marines, the Air Corps, the Army Field Artillery, or the Army Corps of Engineers.

Resistance to black officers persisted, as did black protest against the lack of officer training. Things began to change when Joel Spingarn, the white chairman of the NAACP, lobbied the War Department to establish a training camp for black officers. He was challenged to find two hundred black college students.

By May 1917, the Central Committee of Negro College Men (organized at Howard University) had enrolled fifteen hundred members. On June 15, 1917, the first camp for training and commissioning black officers was established at Fort Des Moines, Iowa, under the command of Major General Charles C. Ballou. Twelve hundred fifty men were admitted, with the majority from the regular Army.

On October 14, 1917, in a historical first, the Army commissioned 639 black officers: 106 captains, 329 first lieutenants, and 204 second lieutenants. They were cheered by blacks nationwide, but not by all whites. When the young second lieutenant George Washington Lee passed through Vicksburg, Mississippi, in uniform, white Mississippi guardsmen gave the rebel yell, and

Lee was warned to leave town as soon as possible. This was far from the only anti-black incident of 1917.

On July 2, 1917, one of the bloodiest race riots in American history broke out: in East St. Louis, Illinois, sparked by white protest against black workers in a factory holding government contracts. Between forty and one hundred blacks were killed over several days, and black homes were set on fire. On July 28, the NAACP led a silent march in New York City. Ten thousand black people—women and children in white, men with black armbands—marched down Fifth Avenue with signs reading: "Mr. President, Why Not Make America Safe for Democracy?" Nearly one hundred blacks, including five women, would be lynched during the nine months that America was at war.

A month after the silent march, what the Army called a mutiny occurred at Camp Logan in Houston, Texas, where black men of the 24th Infantry were regularly insulted and assaulted by local police and civilians.

The "mutiny" began when a black soldier, Private Alonzo Edwards, went to the aid of a black woman being beaten by Houston police and was himself beaten and arrested. Unarmed, like all black MPs in the South, Corporal Charles Baltimore of the 24th Infantry Military Police went to inquire about Edwards—and he, too, was beaten and arrested. When the news of the incidents reached Camp Logan, white officers locked away all weapons. The 24th rebelled, nevertheless. A sergeant was killed, and guns were seized. Led by Sergeant Vida Henry, an eighteen-year veteran of the regiment, 24th Infantry soldiers marched on Houston's police station in company strength. More than a dozen people, including several police officers and four black soldiers, were killed and twelve others were seriously injured. A whole division of Camp Logan's white troops was sent after the black soldiers. Sergeant Vida Henry preferred suicide to capture, but the rest of the men surrendered.

There were several trials. Of the more than one hundred members of the 24th indicted, only a few were acquitted. Of those convicted, 19 were hanged, and more than 80 were sentenced to long prison terms or life imprisonment. Thanks to a NAACP-led campaign for justice, most of the men were free by 1924, with the last man not released until 1938.

The new 92nd Division, formed in late November 1917, was drawn from the first contingent of black draftees arriving in camps around the country at the end of October. The division would contain the 365th, 366th, 367th, and 368th regiments.

On October 26, it had been announced that all officers of general and field rank, including medical officers, would be white, as would all officers attached to division headquarters, except for lieutenants. Organized and trained in five months, the 92nd Division and its new black lieutenants were sent to seven different training camps in Kansas, Iowa, Illinois, Ohio, Maryland, New York, and New Jersey. No other division in the Army was trained in so many different camps. Most black draftees came from the South, and it was the unwritten custom to assign men to camps nearest their homes. In the case of blacks, however, any overlarge concentration was considered dangerous, so thousands of southern black draftees were sent north in the fall of 1917 to train.

The 92nd was poorly trained and poorly led. It never functioned in battle as a division until two days before the Armistice that ended the war. The division and its new black officers were sabotaged from the start by Major General Charles Ballou, the division commander, who warned members of the 92nd not to do "ANYTHING, no matter how legally correct" that would "provoke racial animosity," adding "white men made the Division, and they can break it just as easily if it becomes a trouble maker." Many blacks rightly felt that Ballou's post belonged to Charles Young. In early 1917, Young had been blocked from promotion to full colonel by a bogus medical report that claimed he had high blood pressure and therefore had to retire from the Army. Black America was outraged, starting with black leaders and the press. When the white press began to follow Young's startling nonstop cavalry ride from Ohio to Washington, D.C., to prove his fitness, the Army was forced to blink. Five days before the Armistice, Young was promoted to full colonel, and recalled to active duty with the Ohio National Guard. He never got over missing World War I.

The 92nd received its baptism of fire on August 25, 1918, in the front lines of Saint Die, France. Lieutenant Aaron Fisher of the 366th Regiment received the Distinguished Service Cross, and Lieutenant Thomas Bullock of the 367th became the first black officer of the 92nd Division to die in battle.

That same month, the leader of the American Expeditionary Forces (AEF) in France, General John J. "Blackjack" Pershing, who won his nickname for the color of his troops in the Spanish-American War, had a directive issued to the French Army not to commend black American troops "too highly." This example of official American military racism was ignored by the French, who were said to have burned the directive.

In September, as a 366th Regiment raiding party captured five Germans, two members of the 366th were captured by Germans, who at that point discovered that the 92nd Division was black. The first German propaganda arrived on September 12, in what looked like gas shells.

"Hello boys, what are you doing over here," it read. "Do you enjoy the same rights as white people do in America, the land of freedom and democracy, or are you rather treated over there as second class citizens? . . . To carry a gun in this service is not an honor, but a shame. . . . Throw it away and come over to the German lines. You will find friends who will help you." Not one soldier deserted. The 366th went on to win eighteen Distinguished Service Crosses for the twenty continuous days it spent at the front under terrifying artillery fire. Unfortunately, the reputation of the 92nd Division was damaged that same September, in the Meuse-Argonne offensive.

According to an article in *Harvey's Weekly* in 1919, the 368th had "refused to obey orders" and "did not go forward" when told to attack. The failure to complete the mission was blamed on "the inefficiency and cowardice" of the black company officers. Thirty black officers of the 368th were relieved of command and sent back to America. Five faced courts-martial for cowardice in the face of the enemy. Four were sentenced to death by firing squad; one to life imprisonment. All five officers were later freed, thanks to Captain Leroy Goodman, a black lawyer.

The secretary of war's defense of the 368th was printed in the NAACP's *Crisis* magazine in December 1919. "The circumstances disclosed by a detailed study of the situation . . . afford no basis at all for any of the general assumptions, with regard to the action of colored troops in this battle or elsewhere in France. On the contrary, it is to be noted that many colored officers, and particularly three in the very battalion here under discussion, were decorated with Distinguished Service Crosses for extraordinary heroism under fire."

Howard H. Long, a black first lieutenant, blamed the 368th disaster on the white 2nd Battalion commander—apparently on the verge of a documented nervous breakdown—who lost contact with some of his men.

On November 10 and 11, 1918, in the last battles of the war, twenty-four members of the 365th were commended for meritorious conduct at Bois Fréhaut. Among those who received the Croix de Guerre (War Cross) for that battle was seventeen-year-old Frederick White of Cambridge, Massachusetts, a great-great-great-grandson of the soldier-fifer of the American Revolution Barzillai Lew.

The entire 367th Regiment, said to be the best trained of all draftee regiments in the U.S. Army, was cited for bravery and awarded the Croix de Guerre for its heroic drive toward Metz on November 10 and 11. At the Battle of Metz, they saved the white 56th Regiment from annihilation.

In nine months in France, a total of 103 officers and 1,543 enlisted men of the 92nd were killed in action or died of other causes, such as wounds and disease. Fourteen black officers and forty-three enlisted men of the 92nd received Distinguished Service Crosses.

The second black division, the 93rd, was formed in December 1917. One of its members was Haywood Hall, a member of the black National Guard regiment, the 8th Illinois, which was ordered to Camp Logan in August 1917. (Half the regiment was in place when the 24th Infantry's "mutiny" occurred.)

Hall's father was a self-taught student of black history, particularly black military history. On the living-room wall of the Halls' home in Omaha, Nebraska, hung a Civil War "Remember Fort Pillow!" banner and a print of the 10th Cavalry and 24th Infantry charging up San Juan Hill. Hall's older brother, Otto, wrote a poem about blacks at San Juan Hill that was published in an Omaha daily newspaper.

In 1914, the Halls moved to Minneapolis, Minnesota. There, on Haywood Hall's first day of school, an all-white class singing old plantation songs broadened their accents into jeering drawls when he walked into the room. He turned around, walked out, and never returned to school. At age sixteen, he became a dining-car waiter for the Chicago Northwestern Railway.

At age nineteen, like many of his friends, Hall joined the 8th Illinois. Since the post–Civil War period, all black Guard units had some black officers, but Chicago's 8th Illinois had all black officers, including a black commander, Colonel Franklin A. Denison.

The 8th Illinois won Camp Logan division championships in track, boxing, and baseball. They had the highest number of marksmen, sharpshooters, and expert riflemen. And after six weeks of training, they were ready for France.

The 8th Illinois arrived in Brest on April 16, 1918, with six black field officers, including Colonel Denison—but almost immediately, all black field officers, including Denison, were sent home. The 8th Illinois was renamed the 370th Regiment, bearing the arms and uniforms of the French 59th Division.

In June, the 370th distinguished itself in Saint-Mihiel,

France. In July, they were in the Argonne Forest. There, Corporal Isaac Vally of the 370th was awarded the Distinguished Service Cross for protecting his comrades by covering, with his foot, a hand grenade dropped among them in a trench.

The 370th would be the first Allied troops to break through the Germans' famous system of trenches known as the Hindenburg Line, retaking the fortress town of Laon, some eighty miles northeast of Paris, held by the Germans since 1914. This brave black regiment also fought in the last battle of the war, in Belgium, on the morning of November 11, 1918. Sixty-eight members of the 370th won the Croix de Guerre, and twenty-one received Distinguished Service Crosses, America's second-highest military honor. They went to France with 2,500 men and returned with 1,260.

Equally impressive was the regiment originally named the 15th New York, whose valor was remembered, among other places, in Major Arthur W. Little's book, *From Harlem to the Rhine*. When war was declared, Little, who was white and overaged, tried unsuccessfully to join a white regiment, then offered his services to the 15th New York, a National Guard regiment with mostly white officers.

The 15th, belonging to the biggest and most culturally vibrant black community in America, was known as Harlem's Own. Its black officers and enlisted men reflected Harlem's rich diversity, from its educated middle-class to illiterate migrants newly arrived from the South. Heading the regiment was Colonel William Hayward, veteran of the Spanish-American and Philippine wars. Hayward was determined to make the regiment a success for two reasons: he had a healthy ego, and he believed that black soldiers should be in combat.

The popular press delighted in the regiment's officers. None was as well advertised as Colonel Hayward, but its most celebrated white younger officer was Captain Hamilton "Ham" Fish, Jr., a graduate of Harvard University, where he had been a football star. In his autobiography, *Memoir of an American Patriot*, Fish stated that when Hayward invited him to join the 15th, he accepted "on the spot."

Major Arthur Little was impressed. After all, Ham Fish was a member of a very illustrious New York family, which included Colonel Nicholas Fish, who had fought in the American Revolution and led the enactment of New York State's 1799 gradual emancipation act.

Arthur Little also had words of praise for the 15th's black officers. His highest praise went to the regiment's bandmaster, Lieutenant James Reese Europe, who was born in Alabama and raised in Washington, D.C., where he studied violin with the assistant bandmaster of the U.S. Marine Corps. "A most extraordinary man without qualification or limitation as to race, color, or any other element" was how Little summed up Lieutenant Europe—better known as Jim Europe, orchestra leader, recording star, and national celebrity.

Like most black officers, Europe was educated and middle-class. He had volunteered in order to make a statement about black men as citizens and soldiers. Because Europe was a line officer in charge of a machine-gun unit, the band was strictly in addition to his other duties. And what a band it was. It included Frank De Broit, one of the best cornet players in the world, Bill Robinson (future tap-dance great), and the legendary songwriter-singer Noble Sissle. Europe's band would become a huge sensation at home and abroad.

When Governor Whitman presented the regimental colors in front of the Union League Club in the spring of 1917, there was a big parade. The crowd roared as the colors were marched up Fifth Avenue to Jim Europe's syncopated rendition of "Onward, Christian Soldiers."

In June, the regiment was slighted; Colonel Hayward, "wounded and bitter": the 15th had been denied inclusion in the new "Rainbow Division" of National Guard units. Hayward had been told that black was "not a color of the rainbow." When the 15th was then denied permission to march in the New York National Guard "Farewell to Little Old New York" parade, Hayward told Arthur Little that he "wanted to cry." Hayward vowed that when the war was over, the 15th New York would have the best homecoming parade "that New York will ever have seen."

The 15th New York was officially recognized as part of the U.S. Army on July 15, 1917. Instead of training like other militia, it was divided into small detachments and placed on guard duty in various parts of New York, New Jersey, and Pennsylvania. Colonel Hayward never stopped agitating for combat, and eventually his campaign paid off. In October, the 15th was reassembled and ordered to Camp Wadsworth in Spartanburg, South Carolina, for twelve days of training before departing for France.

"I was sorry to learn that the Fifteenth Regiment has been ordered here . . . for, with their northern ideas about race equality, they will expect to be treated like white men," the mayor of

Spartanburg told *The New York Times*. "I can say right here that they will not be treated as anything except negroes."

The day after the 15th arrived in Spartanburg, Hayward assembled the entire company and urged restraint and self-control. He appealed, "on grounds of self-respect," that the men not go where their presence was "not desired." He warned them not to retaliate in case of physical abuse, but to report every incident, in detail, to him.

The Spartanburg "riot" began on a Sunday morning when Regimental Drum Major Noble Sissle went to the newsstand in the local hotel.

When I went to the stand, I was roughly grabbed in the collar from behind, and before I realized what had happened my service hat was knocked from my head. A gruff voice roared, "Say, nigger, don't you know enough to take your hat off?" . . . I reached for my hat and as I did so received a kick accompanied by an oath. Lost for words, I stammered out: "Do you realize you are abusing a United States soldier and that is a government hat you knocked to the floor?"

"Damn you and the government too," the man replied. "No nigger can come into my place without taking off his hat."

Sissle left as soon as he could, but not before receiving three more kicks.

"Within a few seconds, however, the lobby of that hotel was in an uproar," reported Arthur Little. "Forty or fifty white soldiers, lounging there, had witnessed the outrage." There had already been incidents where white soldiers from New York's 7th Regiment had defended members of the 15th from Spartanburg racists. When Sissle was assaulted, whites from New York's 12th and 71st Regiments were ready to do the same. "But the melee was quelled by a loud cry of 'ATTEN . . . TION!' " Little wrote, followed by an order to leave quietly, singly and in pairs. It was Lieutenant James Reese Europe speaking. The man who had assaulted Sissle turned on Europe, telling him to leave the premises—and cursing him out in the bargain.

Bloodshed was avoided, and later that day Colonel Hayward departed for Washington, D.C., to urge the War Department to remove his men from Spartanburg. On October 24, the 15th was ordered to Camp Whitman, New York. Before the year was out, the regiment set sail for France, with William Layton, a latecomer into their ranks, making the journey.

As a boy, William Layton, whose grandfather had escaped slavery in Virginia via the Underground Railroad and had fought in the Civil War, didn't have dreams of being a professional soldier; he wanted to be a musician. He learned to play the bugle with the Newark Boy Scouts. By age ten, he was playing in Sunday-school concerts and at baseball games. Layton got the notion of being a soldier in the summer of 1917, when he found that all of his friends were enlisting and joining the 15th New York.

At the recruiting station, an officer told seventeen-year-old Layton that he was too short and too skinny. Layton pleaded until the recruiter gave in and told him to drink a quart of milk, eat four bananas, and then come back and be weighed. Layton made the weight but was told he could not join the 15th: they were already organized and on active duty, waiting to go overseas. Instead, he was ordered to join the 24th Infantry in Texas. Layton said no thanks—the 24th Infantry "mutiny" in Brownsville, Texas, was still news. Layton insisted that the only regiment he wanted to join was the 15th. His persistence paid off.

The 15th New York arrived in Brest on an icy New Year's Day, 1918. William Layton soon found himself both chief bugler of Company L and a corporal, and Harlem's Own found themselves designated the 369th.

The winter of 1918, with bitter cold and raging influenza, was known as Valley Forge. Acute shortages of clothing and boots plagued the frontline soldiers. The 369th traveled in unheated railroad cars from Brest to Saint-Nazaire. There, although neither officers nor enlisted men knew anything about handling cargo and construction, they were put to work as stevedores and dam builders. Black stevedores handled the greater percentage of the daily average of over 25,000 tons of cargo.

Saint-Nazaire was a racial war zone between black stevedores and white Marines pressed into stevedore duty. According to William Layton, Saint-Nazaire Marines "began killing black soldiers one by one." The 369th retaliated. "When a black was found dead, they killed a white soldier," Layton said in 1990, of events that were widely believed in but never officially verified.

The military high command decided the answer was to send the 15th to the front. "But no American units would fight with us," Layton said. But French units would. "We'll take 'em, we need 'em," said France's General Ferdinand Foch. And so the 369th was sent to relieve the front lines of General Henri Gouraud's forces at Châlons. The 369th was the first U.S. regiment ever to serve as an integral part of a foreign army. And in May 1918 the regiment's Henry Johnson, of Albany, New York, became the first American enlisted man to win the Croix de Guerre.

In the dark early morning of May 14, Sergeant Johnson and Private Needham Roberts were on guard duty near an American-held bridge on the Aisne River when they heard the sound of wire clippers. Shouting, "Corporal of the Guard!" Johnson and Roberts threw an illuminating rocket—and were immediately hit by a volley of enemy grenades. It was a raiding party of some twenty Germans.

Badly hurt and unable to rise, Roberts propped himself against the door of the dugout and began throwing grenades out into the darkness. Johnson, also wounded, did likewise. Then, armed with only a rifle and a bolo knife, Johnson confronted the enemy soldiers one by one as they entered the narrow enclosure, firing his first three shots at the first German who appeared. With no time to reload, Johnson swung his rifle butt at the next.

Meanwhile, Roberts was almost taken prisoner. But Johnson, leaping like "a wild cat" at the back of Roberts's helmetless captor, buried his bolo knife in the German's scalp. The German soldier whom Johnson had downed with his rifle butt then shot Johnson in the leg with his Lüger automatic. Though hit, Johnson still managed to disembowel his attacker with his knife. His hand-to-hand-combat skills frightened the Germans into retreat. Unbeknownst to Johnson and Roberts, their grenades had killed several Germans. The enemy's retreat would be followed later by "pools of blood."

"The Battle of Henry Johnson," by the renowned war correspondent Irvin Cobb, appeared a few days later on the front page of *The New York World.* By the next morning the Associated Press had spread the story of Henry Johnson all over America. "Our colored volunteers from Harlem," Little wrote, "had become, in a day, one of the most famous fighting regiments of the World War." The Germans named them Hell Fighters.

Johnson and Roberts were both awarded the Croix de Guerre—Johnson's, a higher order, with gold leaf. Both men were cited by General Foch and General John J. Pershing. However, Johnson and Roberts won no official military honors from their own country.

At the end of May, the Germans were at Château-Thierry, less than fifty miles from Paris, and predicting imminent victory. By early June, as Americans began pouring into the lines, the German offensive would be stalled—but by then the French army was demoralized and its men were deserting in droves. In early June, the 369th joined with two U.S. divisions and twenty-five French divisions for the French counterattack at Belleau Wood, a costly Allied victory. In July, the 369th bore the brunt of the German offensive at Minaucourt.

That same month, General Gouraud's troops captured 127 German soldiers and a German officer with plans of the next major attack: an artillery bombardment set for midnight on July 14–15, when it was assumed that the French would be too drunk to respond after celebrating Bastille Day (the national holiday commemorating the start of the French Revolution in 1789). Moments before the scheduled German bombardment, Allied artillery began its own: one of the biggest in military history, with more than 2,500 French and American guns. The Allied counteroffensive was successful. By August, the Allies were winning.

"When the battle had ended thirty percent of my regiment had suffered casualties," wrote Ham Fish of the great Meuse-Argonne offensive of September 26. It was the turning point of the war, and the heaviest fighting for the 369th. All told, the regiment lost about eleven hundred men.

Part of Fish's company was advancing rapidly against the enemy. Information was received that the Germans, planning to attack on both flanks, were leading them into a trap. William Layton was ordered to take a message to Fish, warning him to stop and hold whatever ground was already taken. Layton took off with the message just as the Germans were beginning to lay down an artillery barrage. Scrambling along the banks of the Meuse River, Layton was blown off a hill and gassed, but crawled the rest of the way to deliver the message.

Fish won a Silver Star, and Layton—along with the entire regiment—won the Croix de Guerre. Recovered, Layton rejoined his company for its last engagement, the liberation of Metz. The 369th became the first Allied troops to reach the Rhine.

The 371st Infantry of black South Carolina draftees followed the 369th to France in April 1918. Captain Chester D. Heywood, a white Southerner and officer of the 371st, recalled his experiences with the regiment in *Negro Combat Troops in the World War:*

> *It was a sight never to be forgotten. They came with suit cases and sacks; with bundles and bandanna handkerchiefs full of food, clothing and knick-knacks. Many were barefoot. Some came with guitars and banjos hanging from their backs by strings and ropes.*

Heywood also described the eventual metamorphosis:

> *Clean clothes, well-cooked food in quantity, systematic exercises and drill, regular hours, plus strict but intelligent and helpful discipline, soon worked wonders.*

The 371st definitely became soldiers:

> *The marching and the close-order drill were excellent; the manual of arms unbelievably perfect. The men took the greatest pride in their uniforms and their equipment. Their salutes were snappy; their carriage soldierly; and we were all proud, not only of our individual companies, but of the regiment as a whole.*

In France, the 371st was attached to the famous 157th "Red Hand" Division of the French army, as was another black regiment, the 372nd.

Taking over the trenches of Verdun, the 371st went to the front in June in the Avocourt sector. By then, French soldiers were said to be "sick of the war." They hoped that the Americans would "finish it" in the fall. In September 1918, the 371st prepared to join the Champagne Offensive.

The battle erupted on September 25, in the biggest artillery bombardment in the history of the world. "On the stroke of eleven that night," Heywood wrote, "the whole front for miles seemed to explode in a crashing roar that words cannot describe."

On September 26 and 27, the 371st was poised to attack Hill 188, a former German stronghold, when word came that the enemy wanted to surrender. A German NCO had come into camp, stating that he had thirty-five men who no longer wished "to risk their lives" for a "lost cause."

On September 28, as the 371st moved toward the hill, Germans started climbing onto their trench parapets, their arms held up in surrender. The 371st advanced, then suddenly, a whistle was blown and the Germans jumped back into their trenches and began shooting. The advancing Americans were virtually annihilated.

Corporal Freddie Stowers and his squad continued on in the unrelenting gunfire to destroy the machine-gun station that had inflicted at least 40 percent of his company's casualties. He was on his way, mortally wounded, toward another machine-gun position when he died. Thanks to Corporal Stowers, the new American attack succeeded. The 371st took Hill 188 in three days of battle, but at a price: the regiment lost more than half its men.

Three officers of the 371st received the Legion of Honor; thirty-four officers and eighty-nine enlisted men, the Croix de Guerre; and fourteen officers and twelve men, the American Distinguished Service Cross.

"At exactly 11 o'clock we came out into a clearing and as we did, a rocket went up from the heights behind us. We did not know it at that moment, but this was a signal that the war had ended," wrote Chester D. Heywood of the November 11, 1918, armistice.

Suddenly from the line came a terrific burst of rifle and machine-gun fire and the crash of exploding grenades. We ran forward until we could see the front-line trenches and there standing up on the enemy parapets were groups of Germans yelling, dancing, throwing their little round caps in the air and acting like crazy men. . . . For months we had crouched like animals below ground and now for the first time, we stood up in broad daylight with the enemy in plain sight in front of us. There was no cheering and no display of excitement in our little group. We stood in a dazed silence unable to believe that at last the fighting was over.

In December, General Goybet said farewell to the 371st and 372nd: "Dear friends from America, when you have recrossed the ocean, do not forget the Red Hand Division. Our pure brotherhood in arms has been consecrated in the blood of the brave. These bonds will never be severed." In contrast, within moments of arriving in Brest for the journey home, a 369th private had his head split open by an American military policeman for taking the wrong direction to the latrine. That was not the end of the abuse and disrespect. The 369th may have been the most highly decorated U.S. regiment in the war, but MPs had been instructed not to salute or stand at attention for the 369th's officers, white or black.

The 369th arrived in New York on February 17, 1919, and the homecoming parade up Fifth Avenue was the greatest black American celebration since Emancipation. Officially, it was the homecoming of the entire American Expeditionary Force. But Harlem's Own, in winter overcoats and tin hats, were the first troops to march under the "Victory Arch" at Fifth Avenue and Twenty-fifth Street. America had never seen anything like the wave after wave of black men marching up Fifth Avenue. Major Arthur Little was at the head of the 1st Battalion, about sixty paces behind Jim Europe's band. The reviewing stands were packed, and the sidewalks were overflowing.

At 110th Street and Fifth Avenue, the regiment turned jubilantly into Harlem. Hayward changed the phalanx formation to open-platoon formation. "So far as might be possible," Little wrote, "the face and figure of each soldier boy must be made to stand out, for his loved ones to see and recognize." According to Little, 250,000 black children and adults "went wild with a frenzy of pride and joy and love."

Meanwhile, back in Europe, black soldiers were feeling anything but victorious. For one, black troops were made to do much of the war's cleanup. Nine thousand black soldiers had the job of reburying all the dead, with white soldiers as clerks.

"We regret that on October 1919 we will sail for our home in Petersburg, Va. United States of America where true democracy is enjoyed only by the white people," wrote a black private, William Hewlett, on August 26, 1919, to the editor of the *Crisis* magazine, W.E.B. Du Bois. "Why did black men die here in France 3300 miles from their home? Was it to make democracy safe for the white people in America, with the black race left out?"

Within four months of the 369th Regiment's triumphal Fifth Avenue parade, there were race wars in the streets of America. The summer of 1919 became known as Red Summer—"Red" for blood. Seventy-eight blacks were lynched in 1919: ten were veterans, several of whom were lynched in uniform. By the end of the year, there had been race riots in twenty-eight cities, North and South.

On the night of July 28, 1919, in the midst of the Chicago

race riot, Haywood Hall and other black veterans met at the 370th Regimental Armory. "It was rumored that Irishmen from west of the Wentworth Avenue dividing line were planning to invade the ghetto that night," Hall recalled years later. "We planned a defensive action to meet them." Fortunately for the Irish, the invasion never occurred. The "defensive action" of the 370th centered around the use of Army-issue 1903 Springfield rifles and a Browning submachine gun.

The Red Summer was red in politics as well as blood. The Wilson administration had been terrified by the Russian Revolution, which began in 1917, and ended in victory for the Communists—called Reds—who would create the Soviet Union, a federation of more than a dozen Communist republics. In 1919, the Palmer Raids—named for the U.S. attorney general, A. Mitchell Palmer, but directed by J. Edgar Hoover—initiated a systematic decade-long persecution of all shades of the American left. One of the left's new soldiers was Haywood Hall.

"The Chicago rebellion of 1919 was a pivotal point in my life," Hall wrote in his autobiography, *Black Bolshevik* (under the name Harry Haywood). "Always I had been hot-tempered and never took any insults lying down. This was even more true after the war." Influenced by his brother, Otto, also a veteran, he stepped into the class war: he joined Otto in the Communist Party.

In January 1920, the *Crisis* magazine reprinted a letter from a Dr. John Hugh Reynolds, written to *The Arkansas Gazette* about men like Hall:

We have a new Negro; he has come back from the war changed. . . . He has taken much credit to himself for our

victory, and he has come back with a new sense of his impor-
tance and with aspirations, the realization of which means to
overturn our traditional views and modes of life. A cardinal
fact is that the Negro is not willing to take his old place and
status before the war. In some cases he has come back with
ideas of social and political equality.

THE SPANISH CIVIL WAR

> *We didn't know too much about the Spaniards, but we knew that they were fighting against fascism, and that fascism was the enemy of all black aspirations.*
>
> —Vaughn Love, veteran of the Spanish Civil War

After World War I, there was a new sense of disillusion and a widespread feeling that democracy had failed. For many, especially in Europe, only the new orders of Fascism and Communism offered any hope for the future.

Fascism and Communism are both forms of totalitarianism (a government with practically total control of all aspects of a society). Communism, which promised that all the resources of a nation would be owned collectively by all the people (and thus wealth would be more fairly distributed), gave hope to masses of people who felt exploited by the wealthy few. Unlike Communism, Fascism proclaimed that people of a certain race or ethnicity should be a nation unto themselves. This appealed to people who hated ethnic minorities and "foreigners" in their country (and often blamed them for their nation's problems). Meanwhile, in America racism remained strong. In 1924, the Ku Klux Klan had 4.5 million members.

The Great Depression (1929–1939) was a gift to the Communist movement. In a decade that saw southern blacks lynched at the rate of one every three weeks, Communism appeared to address the twin problems of racism and economic oppression more forcefully than the NAACP. Black membership in the Communist Party U.S.A. (CPUSA) was low, but the party's influence was high. The small CPUSA would compete with the NAACP throughout the 1930s.

Millions of ordinary black Americans insisted that it was possible to be "progressive" without being a Communist, to be pro-labor without being anti-capitalist, and to change America without a revolution. The ideas and the times came together in President Franklin Delano Roosevelt's New Deal, a peaceful political revolution that began in 1932.

The New Deal created government programs that became better known by their acronyms. These programs included the WPA (Works Progress Administration, which hired jobless artists and artisans); CCC (Civilian Conservation Corps, which employed jobless youth); NYA (National Youth Administration, for young women and men); FDIC (Federal Deposit Insurance Corporation, to guarantee bank deposits); HOLC (Home Owners Loan Corporation, to save homes from foreclosures); and SEC (Securities and Exchange Commission, to ensure truth in the sale of stocks and bonds). The New Deal also gave birth to Social Security and unemployment insurance.

President Roosevelt, struck by polio at the age of thirty-nine, became a giant of history. The man commonly referred to by his initials, FDR, had enough confidence and charisma to convince Americans to have faith in the New Deal. Most Americans, including blacks, were getting behind FDR, as much because of his wife (and cousin), Eleanor, friend to the poor and oppressed of every color, as because of his new economic programs.

FDR's administration had more black political appointees than any before it in American history. Roosevelt also had more black advisers than any president before him. There was an unofficial "Black Cabinet" (the Federal Council on Negro Affairs), headed up by Mary McLeod Bethune, director of Negro Affairs for the New Deal's National Youth Administration. Other members of the Black Cabinet included tennis champion Edgar Brown, who served as adviser in the Civilian Conservation Corps; Lawrence Oxley, of the Division of Negro Labor in the U.S. Department of Labor; William Hastie, NAACP lawyer (and future first black federal judge), who was assistant solicitor in the Department of the Interior; and my great-uncle, Dr. Frank Horne, an adviser in federal housing programs.

The Black Cabinet gave blacks a theoretical voice in nearly every New Deal program, although it was usually ignored when programs were put into practice in the South. Nevertheless, by the end of the 1930s, 300,000 black youths were involved in National Youth Administration training programs; 250,000 were in the Civilian Conservation Corps; and the WPA was providing basic earnings for one million black families.

Eleanor Roosevelt also helped blacks get a fairer share of the New Deal. On an inspection tour of southern New Deal programs, she found widespread discrimination against blacks. In 1935, thanks to his wife's prodding, FDR signed an executive order barring discrimination in all WPA projects. Despite hostility in many quarters of the administration, Mrs. Roosevelt found allies, but she also inspired suspicion. In the autumn of 1935, a photograph of Mrs. Roosevelt accepting a bouquet of roses from a five-year-old black girl triggered an avalanche of hate propaganda in the South, denouncing her as a "Communist." This was all good for the black vote, which, by the 1936 election, was entirely FDR's.

The military had no intention of giving blacks a new deal.

The four Buffalo Soldier regiments were being downsized. Many black companies were abolished or converted from combat units to service units. As for the Navy, with the end of World War I, blacks were eligible only for the stewards' branch.

America as a nation was not officially involved in any war between the first and second world wars, but individual Americans were: in the struggle against Fascism abroad.

Spain's Fascists had assumed an easy takeover during the simmering civil war that followed the exile of King Alfonso XIII in 1931. After King Alfonso's departure, Spain was ruled by the anti-Fascist Provisional Government of the Republic of Spain. And in the election of February 1936, the Popular Front beat the Fascist National Front.

Broadly speaking, the Popular Front, unlike the National Front, wanted to change Spain. Members of the Popular Front coalition ranged from liberals who simply wanted to pull the country out of feudal monarchism (the intellectual elite and free-thinking city-dwellers) to those who wanted some sort of revolution (trade unionists, mostly miners), and those with a special grievance (Catalan and Basque nationalists). Spain's small Communist Party was only one of several on the anti-Fascist left, among whom the Socialists were particularly strong.

The Popular Front's triumph over the National Front was challenged several months after the election by General Francisco Franco, former chief of staff of the Spanish army. Franco, a Fascist, had been banished to the Canary Islands right after the election for declaring war on the Popular Front, known as the Republicans.

On July 18, 1936, Franco attacked the southern mainland with the Spanish army of North Africa. This army was composed of Moroccan troops who had served under Franco. They were ferried to Cádiz by German transport planes in response to a plea from Franco to Germany's Chancellor Adolf Hitler, whose Fascism was even more extreme than Franco's.

While Franco had taken the southern cities of Córdoba and Seville and most of northwest Spain, his rebellion had failed in most of the major cities. With Franco nearing Madrid, the country's political and geographical center, the government of the Spanish Republic was moved to Valencia, on the Mediterranean coast. Most of southeast and central Spain and the Mediterranean cities of Barcelona and Valencia were still in Republican hands. The life of the Republic depended on Madrid, Barcelona, and Valencia, whose military units had remained loyal.

Franco's military advantage soon became enormous. To the approximately 80 percent of the Spanish army who joined the rebellion were added ten thousand Germans, two divisions from Antonio Salazar's Portugal, and a hundred thousand Italian troops fresh from Ethiopia. (In the fall of 1935, in the first step in his plan to conquer Europe, Italy's Fascist dictator, Benito Mussolini, had sent his "African Legions" to take Ethiopia. In May 1936, Italian troops captured Addis Ababa, the capital of Ethiopia, and Mussolini proclaimed, "At last Italy has her empire!")

Desperate for arms, the Spanish government appealed to the international community for arms sales. But the League of Nations nonintervention pact of August 1936 (which Germany and Italy ignored) forbade the sale of arms to Spain. The democracies, which basically hoped that Fascism and Communism would cancel each other out, remained neutral. The U.S. Congress passed the Neutrality Act, making it a crime for any U.S. citizen to go to Spain.

Only Socialist Mexico, Czechoslovakia, and the Soviet Union sold arms and/or matériel to Spain. The Soviet Union also sent some two thousand military advisers. That the vastly outmanned and outmachined Spanish Republic lasted three years was owed, foremost, to the heroism of the Spanish people and, secondarily, to material aid from the Soviet Union; but it was also owed, in great part, to the International Brigades, multinational volunteer forces composed of people who hated Fascism. Volunteers came from a range of nations, including Germany, Italy, the Balkans, France, and Belgium. These volunteers would come to give the fist-to-temple Popular Front salute, greet each other with *"Salud!"* ("Health!") and call each other "Comrade." The five International brigades and the battalions within them took names associated with a freedom struggle. For instance, the 12th Garibaldi Brigade of Italian anti-Fascists was named for a nineteenth-century revolutionary. The Balkan 13th Dabrowsky Brigade was named for an early-nineteenth-century Polish freedom fighter.

The English-speaking 15th Brigade (plus an attached unit of Spanish-speaking volunteers from Latin America) was essentially four separate battalions—British, Canadian, Irish, and American. The Americans voted to call themselves the Abraham Lincoln Battalion. At one point or another, American units included the George Washington Battalion, the John Brown and Frederick Douglass Field Artillery Companies, and the Tom Mooney Machine Gun Company. (The labor leader Tom Mooney was serving a life sentence for a 1916 bombing, for which he would be pardoned and released in 1939.)

Some 2,800 American men and women—numbers vary because of aliases—joined the Lincolns. Approximately nine hundred were Jewish; eighty to one hundred were black. Most of the white volunteers had no military training, but many blacks, older than the brigade's average of twenty-three, were World War I or National Guard veterans, and most were Communists.

American volunteers were a diverse group. They included a large contingent of merchant seamen; a ballet dancer; a Texas Ranger; three self-described acrobats; the sons of a former governor of Ohio and of a mayor of Los Angeles; the brother of a congressman from Wisconsin; James Lardner, son of sports reporter turned short-story writer Ring Lardner; and a Japanese American, Jack Shirai, from San Francisco, who became the Lincolns' cook.

The first group of American volunteers left New York the day after Christmas, 1936. With tickets paid for by Communist organizations (and orders to talk to no one but their cabinmates) they sailed third class on the *Normandie,* queen of the French Line. France, which shares a border with Spain, was officially neutral, but Prime Minister Léon Blum was a Socialist, and his government was Popular Front. Thus, early on, volunteers could easily reach Spain through France. At Le Havre, the French customs officers, seeing camping gear, hiking boots, and leather jackets, passed the volunteers' bags with the Popular Front salute.

After a stay in Paris, the first volunteer group proceeded by train to Perpignan, near the Spanish border. Later volunteers, after the French border was closed, faced the terrifying eight-hour night climb over the Pyrenees Mountains—where most of the new camping gear was tossed away.

*   *   *

Twenty-seven-year-old Captain Robert Hale Merriman was the first commander of the Abraham Lincolns. Merriman, a economics teacher from Berkeley, had a second lieutenant's commission from the University of Nevada ROTC. For help turning the Lincolns into soldiers, Merriman looked to the few men among them with military experience, including black volunteers Oliver Law, a veteran of a Buffalo Soldier regiment (the 24th Infantry) and Walter Garland. Law and Garland became machine-gun section leaders, in charge of two of the company's four 1914 Soviet-made Maxim machine guns.

"More serious than jovial," one Lincoln wrote of Oliver Law, "but never harsh; he was well-liked by his men. . . . It was spoken of him that he was calm under fire, dignified, respectful of his men and always given to thoughtful consideration of initiatives and military missions."

Twenty-three-year-old Walter Garland, a former member of New York's 369th Regiment and a Harlem Communist Party activist, was also thought well of. Milton Wolff, a white art student from Brooklyn who became the last Lincoln commander, called Garland a "machine-gunner extraordinaire." Wolff, known as El Lobo (The Wolf), credited Garland with teaching him everything he knew about the Maxim machine gun.

The most popular black Lincoln was the adopted son of the celebrated white photographer Consuelo Kanaga: dark, chubby-faced Eluard McDaniels, the sometime art student, longshoreman, and baseball player. Twenty-five-year-old McDaniels was known as El Fantastico because of his amazing grenade pitching. Many Spaniards loyal to the Republic regarded all the Lincolns as Fantasticos. The Lincolns became the most popular Internationals, with the entire 15th Brigade fixed in the public imagination through the song "Viva la Quince Brigada!" ("Long Live the 15th Brigade!").

By February 1937, Madrid was in true danger. Fascists were about to cross the Jarama River, key to its southern defense. The Republican air force successfully took on German aircraft, but superior Fascist ground forces were defeating poorly trained British, French, and Balkan volunteers. Having spent a month drilling without rifles and ammunition, the Lincolns were called in as reinforcements. Many saw their first weapon the day they went into battle, on February 23, in an olive grove near Jarama's Pingarron Hill.

They had been ordered to lead the attack on Pingarron—without air or artillery support. Merriman let each man take five practice shots at the side of a hill with their new Soviet-made rifles. "Many got wounded just as they climbed the parapet to go over," remembered Pingarron veteran John Tisa. "Some comrades from among the recent arrivals, uninformed and inexperienced, went over the top with full packs on their backs and charged toward the Fascists." Of the 500 Lincolns who went into battle, many were wounded, and 127 were killed. The Fascists lost and retook Pingarron Hill three times. During the monthlong battle, Republicans and Fascists each had about ten thousand casualties, or 25 percent losses.

After Pingarron, the twice-wounded Walter Garland was promoted to lieutenant, as was Oliver Law.

*   *   *

Vaughn Love and James Yates were two of the five black Americans who sailed to France on February 20, 1937, with the largest contingent of Americans heading for Spain (three hundred out of eight hundred passengers). "Although we talked with each other and played poker," Vaughn Love later recalled, "we all kept our destination a secret." Love was the son of a World War I medical-corps officer and godson of World War I hero Sergeant Henry Johnson.

"We were all deep revolutionaries," Love said in a later interview. "We thought, 'We have to get to the front and kill these Fascists!' . . . I was through with the system. I knew it didn't work, and I was thinking in terms of changing society—to change the world." In Spain, Love joined the Washington Battalion, formed after the Battle of Pingarron as more Americans arrived. Its captain was Oliver Law, a friend of James Yates.

James Yates, who left his native Mississippi for Chicago only two or three steps ahead of the Klan, was a railway union organizer. Moving to New York, Yates joined the Communist Party—and saw his Chicago and Harlem friends, Oliver Law and Walter Garland among them, leave for Spain without him. Yates had trouble getting a passport because Mississippi did not keep records of black births.

In Paris, Yates shared a hotel room with a Swede, an English Jew, and a Nazi-hating German. He was "learning so much about people, and the world," he later wrote, that he felt his head would "split wide open." Yates found Paris's most famous and glorious avenue, the Champs-Élysées, and couldn't believe that he, "a poor fellow from Mississippi," was actually there. But "painful memories of being constantly rejected" in his own country kept him from going into a café. Yates knew that he had to get over feeling like "half a man." How could he face bullets in Spain if he "couldn't face a café filled with French people"?

Yates conquered the café and, three days later, crossed the Pyrenees. Like most of the volunteers, he lightened his load during the climb. "When it came to my books—three battered paperbacks by Claude McKay, Maxim Gorky, and Langston Hughes—I paused," wrote Yates. "I tried to fit them into my pockets, but they felt like pieces of lead. I fingered them regretfully, then pulled two out, letting them drop. They filtered down through the blackness. It was like a part of me falling." He had kept Langston Hughes.

Jarama and Pingarron had saved the Madrid-Valencia road, but Madrid was still surrounded on three sides. Brunete, a Fascist-held area some nineteen miles west of the capital, saw the first Republican offensive of the war. Its purpose was to relieve Madrid. Supported by over a hundred tanks and a hundred aircraft from the Soviet Union, British and American fighters spearheaded the July 5, 1937, attack. It would be a thirty-day battle—street by street, house by house—in hundred-degree heat.

The Fascists had new troops and firepower. Brunete was a major defeat, and Americans suffered 50 percent casualties. Within days the Washingtons disbanded, and the two decimated units became one new Abraham Lincoln Brigade, with Captain Oliver Law as commander.

On July 10, Law was shot in the stomach as he led an assault in the middle of a wheat field at Brunete's Mosquito Ridge. New Yorker Harry Fisher was there:

I heard the cries for first aid and the moans of the wounded and dying. . . . [Oliver Law] was about twenty yards ahead of us, standing there yelling and waving his pistol. "O.K., fellahs, let's go! Let's go! Let's keep it up. We can chase them off that hill. We can TAKE that hill. Come on!" He got hit just about then. That was the last I saw of him.

To Fisher, it seemed that all the bullets were aimed directly at Law: "You could see the dust rising around him, where hundred[s] of bullets seemed to be converging." Law's friend Jerry Weinberg crawled out and pulled him to the rear. He was placed on a stretcher under protest, and died soon after. His body was buried below Mosquito Ridge, marked with a piece of wood stating his age and race, and hung with his helmet.

Vaughn Love was cited for conspicuous bravery at Brunete and sent to officers' training school. Walter Garland, wounded twice at Jarama, was shot in the knee at Brunete while going to the aid of a fallen comrade. "It was his inspiring leadership that made it possible for us to survive the 21 hellish days of Brunete and go on from there," noted Milt Wolff.

In August 1937, with Lincolns in the vanguard, the Republicans launched a diversionary offensive on the Aragon front, northeast of Madrid. Their mission was to draw Fascist fire away from Bilbao, the Basque capital. Fierce fighting continued in central Spain in defense of Madrid and in the province of Catalonia, whose capital, Barcelona, would become a last lifeline.

At Aragon, black Americans saw action in the air for the first time. Paul Williams and James Peck were two of the thirty-one

Americans trained by Soviets to fly with "La Gloriosa," the collective name of the Republican airmen based around Madrid and Barcelona to protect those cities.

Paul Williams, who had gotten his pilot's license in his home state of Ohio, was a successful aeronautical engineer who had also served in the Navy for a time. Williams's grandfather had served in the Union Navy in the Civil War; his great-great-grandfather had fought with the Navy in the War of 1812; and an earlier ancestor, Jacob Peterson, had helped capture the turncoat Benedict Arnold during the American Revolution.

Peck was a commercial pilot and aviation writer for white periodicals (his race went unmentioned) whose applications to both the Army and Navy flying schools had been rejected. Peck was one of America's three aces. He got four of his five verified kills on the Aragon front.

Autumn brought victory and defeat on the Aragon front, but the severe winter of 1937–1938 saw a dreadful defeat at Teruel, north of Valencia. Teruel marked the beginning of the end of the Republic.

The Battle of Teruel, fought from December 1937 through February 1938, was another diversionary offensive to draw Fascists away from Barcelona. The soldiers fought in a blizzard with subzero temperatures. Some had frostbitten fingers and toes that were later amputated. Like Brunete, the Battle of Teruel began with early Republican victories but became a major defeat. More than fifteen thousand Republicans were killed or injured. Several International brigades, including the Lincolns, suffered heavy losses.

In March 1938, the International Retreats began at the towns of Belchite and Caspe, west of Barcelona, across the other side of the Ebro River. Facing a full-scale Fascist onslaught, Lincolns were the last to leave Caspe. The wild retreat across the Ebro was like a terrible dream—some Internationals, among them Major Robert Merriman, simply disappeared and were assumed to have been killed or captured. A lucky few made it across the river. "There wasn't a man who made the trip who didn't feel death walking by his side," wrote Milt Wolff, the last American to cross.

By late summer 1938, there were three thousand Internationals left. On October 4, 1938, the Republican prime minister, Juan Negrín, officially withdrew the International brigades from Spain. Two thousand Internationals, including Captain Milt Wolff and two hundred other Americans, marched through flower-strewn streets on October 29 at the Barcelona farewell parade.

"The people's salutation knew no bounds," wrote a Lincoln volunteer in a letter home. "Girls broke through the lines and showered us with kisses. . . . The Negro comrades just couldn't march. They were actually besieged! Planes swooped down almost touching the tree-tops and threw leaflets with greetings to the Internationals." People shouted, *"Viva los Internacionales!"* and soldiers shouted, *"Viva la República!"*

Lincolns had a great sense of togetherness. Most returned to America in groups. For James Yates, it was a return to Jim Crow. The Lincolns walked out en masse when their New York City hotel refused to admit him. "I was doubly shocked to be hit so quickly," Yates wrote in his memoir, *Mississippi to Madrid.* "The pain went as deep as any bullet could have done. I had the dizzy feeling that I was back in the trenches again. But this was another front. I was home."

When "home" entered World War II in late 1941, surviving members of the Abraham Lincoln Brigade offered themselves as a unit to the U.S. government. Had their offer not been rejected, theirs would have been the only nonsegregated unit in the American military.

Several hundred Lincolns ended up joining the U.S. armed forces, with James Yates, Walter Garland, and Vaughn Love among them. James Yates joined the Signal Corps and was the only one pulled out of his outfit to stay in America when the unit went overseas. Walter Garland, as a member of the 731st Military Police Battalion at Fort Wadsworth, Staten Island, taught map-making, mortar, and machine guns. He also developed a new machine-gun sighting device, which the Army used. All of Garland's requests for combat duty were denied.

Vaughn Love joined the Quartermaster Corps. After one week of basic training at Camp Lee, Virginia, he became an acting corporal. Within two weeks he was a regimental guard, with a citation for action above the call of duty. Remaining at Camp Lee after basic, he became a sergeant in charge of the only platoon not led by a second lieutenant. He was also assigned to lecture staff officers on ground-troop defense against air and mechanized attack. Love eventually went overseas during World War II, landing at Normandy's "Red Dog" Beach on D-Day.

WORLD WAR II

The V for victory sign is being displayed prominently in all so-called democratic countries . . . then let we colored Americans adopt the double VV for a double victory. The first V for victory over our enemies from without, the second V for victory over our enemies from within. For surely those who perpetuate these ugly prejudices here are seeking to destroy our democratic form of government just as surely as the Axis forces.

—James G. Thompson, a cafeteria worker at Cessna Aircraft, in a letter written in January 1942 to *The Pittsburgh Courier*

On September 1, 1939, Adolf Hitler's Nazi Germany invaded Poland. In reaction, Britain and France declared war on Germany. World War II had begun.

By May 1940, having already taken Peking, Shanghai, Nanking, and Hangchou, Japan was determined to conquer all of China. China's Nationalist leader Chiang Kai-shek had joined forces with the Communists Mao Tse-tung and Chou En-lai against the common foe.

Germany seemed equally unstoppable: it controlled Central and Eastern Europe and the Netherlands, Belgium, and Luxembourg, and was about to take France, where the entire British Expeditionary Forces (BEF), their backs to the sea, were trapped in the north at Dunkirk. In a miraculous nine-day amphibious evacuation, a military-civilian armada of pleasure boats, fishing boats, tugs, and battleships saved the beleaguered BEF. In August, Germany launched an air attack on Britain. "We shall defend our island, whatever the cost may be," declared Britain's Prime Minister Winston Churchill, with the clarion fervor that helped sustain the country through the worst of the Battle of Britain (which lasted until October 1940).

When war broke out in Europe, most Americans were more focused on President Franklin Delano Roosevelt's campaign for a third term.

Many Americans wanted their nation to stay out of the war, but they had begun to understand that they would soon be in it. FDR gave the order for rearmament in the summer of 1940. Late that summer, while Congress debated the new Selective Service Act, the NAACP led a drive against discrimination in the military. The 230,000-man peacetime U.S. Army had fewer than 5,000 blacks, and only 5 of these were officers. Three of the black officers were chaplains. The father-son duo of Colonel Benjamin O. Davis, Sr., and Captain Benjamin O. Davis, Jr., were the sole line officers.

Senator Robert Wagner, a Democrat from New York, introduced an amendment declaring that no one could be denied the right to volunteer because of creed or color. New York's Republican Representative Hamilton Fish, formerly Captain Fish of World War I's Harlem's Own (the 369th regiment), introduced another amendment outlawing discrimination in the selection and training of men. And Howard University professor Rayford W. Logan, chair of the integrated Committee on the Participation of Negroes in the National Defense, reiterated black demands for "equal opportunity" and black military service "in proportion to their numerical strength in the whole population." At the time, there were roughly 13 million blacks in a total population of close to 131 million.

The military establishment remained opposed to equal opportunity for blacks in the armed forces and managed to circumvent Wagner's and Fish's nondiscriminatory language. In its final form, the Selective Service Act stated that no man would be inducted unless he was "acceptable" to the Army and "until adequate provision shall be made for shelter, sanitary facilities, medical care and hospital accommodations." "Acceptable" could mean anything, and "adequate provision" meant segregation. When FDR signed the act on September 14, 1940, blacks flocked to recruitment centers only to be turned away because the Army had too few segregated facilities.

Later that fall a White House meeting was arranged to discuss discrimination in the military. Walter White, head of the NAACP; labor leader A. Philip Randolph, head of one of the most influential black organizations, the Brotherhood of Sleeping Car Porters; and T. Arnold Hill, former secretary of the Urban League, met with Assistant Secretary of War Robert Patterson; Secretary of the Navy Frank Knox; and the president. White and Randolph pressed for the end of segregation in the armed forces.

On October 9, FDR's press secretary, Steve Early, announced the official new government policy on blacks in the Army and Navy. It gave with one hand and took away with the other. Yes, black strength in the Army would reflect the percentage of blacks in the population. Yes, black combat and noncombat units would be organized in every branch of the service, including the formerly barred-to-blacks Air Corps and Marines. Yes, blacks would have the opportunity to attend officer training schools. But all officers in present and future black units, except for three existing black regiments, would be white. And although blacks and whites would enjoy equality of service, they would not be integrated into the same regiments because that would "produce situations destructive to morale and detrimental to the preparation for national defense."

Roosevelt faced a race-relations crisis in the election of 1940, when 19 percent of black men were still unemployed and some had come to refer to the New Deal as the "Dirty Deal." Many responded favorably to the Republican presidential candidate, Wendell Willkie. The 1940 Republican platform pledged that "discrimination must cease" and that blacks "be given a square deal in the economic and political life of this nation." In the end, support for FDR remained strong among blacks and other Americans. On January 20, 1941, he officially began his third term as president. Meanwhile, abroad, war raged on.

February 1941 was a horrible time for Britain. At home, the Royal Air Force (RAF) valiantly confronted Germany's Air Force, the Luftwaffe. British civilians suffered relentless aerial bombardment. Abroad, Tommies (as British soldiers were called) faced Germany's famous, and so far victorious, Afrika Korps in North Africa. In Asia, Hong Kong was poised to fall to the Japanese.

FDR came to the rescue with the Lend-Lease Act of March 1941. This act allowed him to transfer munitions and supplies to "the government of any country whose defense the President deems vital to the defense of the U.S." Lend-Lease not only gave eleventh-hour support to the British, it also enabled the defeat of the Germans in Russia by financing the pivotal Red Army victory at Stalingrad.

Lend-Lease led to a seemingly overnight conversion of American factories, plants, and other business entities from peacetime to wartime production. In this defense industry boom, discrimination was very much in force.

Detail of John Trumbull's *The Battle of Bunker's Hill* (1786).

This painting, *The Flutist*, was once thought to be of fifer-soldier Barzillai Lew, but is now believed to be of his son, Barzillai Lew, Jr., whose descendants fought in every major American military engagement from the Civil War to Vietnam.

French sublieutenant Jean-Baptiste-Antoine de Verger's watercolor *American Foot Soldiers, Yorktown Campaign* (1781), which features a light infantryman of the 1st Rhode Island, the only all-black regiment in the Continental Army.

U.S. Miltary History Institute

The first black recipient of the Medal of Honor, Sergeant William Carney of the 54th Massachusetts. Carney is shown here with the flag he rescued from his fallen commander, Colonel Robert Gould Shaw, in the battle at Fort Wagner in July 1863.

Moorland Spingarn Research Center, Howard University

Sergeant Major Lewis Douglass of the 54th Massachusetts, the eldest son of abolitionist Frederick Douglass.

Library of Congress

A unit of the 107th U.S. Colored Infantry, which took part in the crucial capture of Fort Fisher in January 1865.

The United States Military Academy

Lieutenant Henry Ossian Flipper, the first black graduate of West Point (1877).

Collection of William Loren Katz

Sergeant Horace W. Bivens of the 10th Cavalry, with his famous messenger dog, Booth.

Members of the 10th Cavalry after the charge of San Juan Hill in July 1898.

Cavalryman Lieutenant Benjamin O. Davis in 1907. In 1940, Davis became the first black general in the U.S. military. During World War II, his son, Benjamin O. Davis, Jr., would lead America's first black fighter pilots.

My great-uncle Lieutenant Errol Horne in World War I.

The French citation for the 369th's Sergeant Henry Johnson and Private Needham Roberts, who received the Croix de Guerre for their heroics during a German ambush in May 1918.

A poster featuring band leader Lieutenant James Reese Europe of the 369th Regiment.

Decorated members of the 369th Regiment ("Harlem's Own") returning home.

Heywood K. Butt, William Layton, and Hamilton Fish, among the last surviving members of the 369th Regiment, photographed in 1987.

Vaughn Love, a veteran of the Abraham Lincoln Brigade.

Captain Oliver Law, commander of the Abraham Lincoln Brigade, overseeing an operation just before he was killed during the Brunete campaign in July 1937.

Dorie Miller, hero of Pearl Harbor and the first black recipient of the Navy Cross.

Collection of William Miles

U.S. Army photo

The first class of Tuskegee Airmen in 1942: George "Spanky" Roberts, Benjamin O. Davis, Jr., Charles H. DeBow, Lieutenant R. H. "Mother" Long (advanced flight instructor), Mac Ross, and Lemuel Custis.

My mother, Lena Horne, at Tuskegee in 1943 with members of the ground crew.

General Benjamin O. Davis, Sr., pinning the Distinguished Flying Cross on his son, Colonel Benjamin O. Davis, Jr., in September 1944.

Captain Lee "Buddy" Archer in the cockpit of his plane, *Ina, the Macon Belle,* named after his future wife. In World War II, Archer became America's first black ace.

Charity Adams, the first black major in the Women's Army Corps, having her silver oak leaves pinned on in September 1943. During World War II, Major Adams was the highest-ranking and most important black woman in the U.S. military.

Lieutenant Harriet Pickens, one of the first two black WAVES (Women Accepted for Volunteer Emergency Service).

The first black officers in the U.S. Navy—"The Golden Thirteen." From left to right, top row: John W. Reagan, Jesse W. Arbor, Dalton L. Baugh, Frank C. Sublett. Second row: Graham E. Martin, Charles B. Lear, Phillip S. Barnes, Reginald Goodwin. Third row: James E. Hare, Samuel E. Barnes, George Cooper, W. Sylvester White, Dennis D. Nelson II.

Sergeant Gilbert "Hashmark" Johnson, one of the first black Marine Corps drill instructors, surveying a platoon of recruits in April 1943.

Members of the Marine Corps' 51st Defense Battalion at Eniwetok in the South Pacific in 1945. The 155mm artillery gun is the one they named the *Lena Horne*.

Courtesy of Gene Doughty

Marine Gene Doughty, squad leader and acting platoon sergeant of the 8th Ammunition Company, celebrated his twenty-first birthday on Iwo Jima, where he witnessed the famous raising of the American flag over Mount Suribachi.

Sixteen-year-old E. G. McConnell, who became a member of the 761st Tank Corps, whose motto was "Come Out Fighting."

Courtesy of E. G. McConnell

Troops of Company G, 24th Infantry, ready to move to the firing lines on July 18, 1950. Two days later, in the battle of Yechon, they achieved the first victory of the Korean War.

Members of the mortar platoon of Company M, 24th Infantry, shortly before their regiment was deactivated (October 1, 1951), marking the end of segregation in the U.S. Army.

America's first black four-star general, Daniel "Chappie" James, who served in World War II, Korea, and Vietnam.

This portrait of Colonel Fred V. Cherry, who was a prisoner of war for eight years, hangs in the Pentagon.

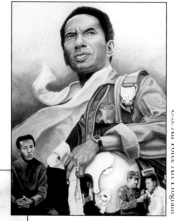

U.S. Air Force Art Program

Courtesy of George Forrest

Lieutenant Colonel George Forrest, whose famous football-trained six-hundred-yard run through enemy fire kept his unit from being overrun in the battle at Ia Drang in November 1965.

Henri Huet, Wide World Photos

Black and white troops continued to share combat as well as comradeship after Ia Drang. These 1st Cavalry Division troops saw heavy fighting in 1966.

General H. Norman Schwarzkopf's war room in Riyadh, Saudi Arabia. Left to right: General Colin Powell, chair of the Joint Chiefs of Staff; Richard Cheney, secretary of defense; Schwarzkopf; and Lieutenant General Cal Waller, deputy commander of Desert Storm.

General Powell visiting the troops in Saudi Arabia during Desert Shield.

Major Flossie Satcher.

Epilogue

In January 1997, seven black winners of the Distinguished Service Cross in World War II received Medals of Honor. Vernon Baker was the sole living recipient. "The only thing that I can say to those who are not with me," he said, "is thank you, fellas, well done. And I will always remember you."

Lieutenant Vernon Baker.

Vernon Baker receiving his Medal of Honor in 1997.

"Negroes will be considered only as janitors," announced the general manager of North American Aviation in the spring of 1941.

"We have not had a Negro working in 25 years and do not plan to start now," stated Standard Steel.

"It is not the policy of this company to employ other than of the Caucasian race," said California's Vultee Air.

In response to blacks being shut out of defense industry jobs, A. Philip Randolph mobilized his troops. He began organizing a march on Washington, scheduled for July 1, 1941. By the first week of June, there were march committees in eighteen cities, North and South.

FDR and First Lady Eleanor Roosevelt were sympathetic to Randolph's demands, but they were firmly opposed to the March on Washington. They asked him repeatedly to call it off, fearing that it would create "even more solid opposition" from certain groups in Congress. But Randolph continued to mobilize for July 1. Then, on June 18, Randolph and Walter White met with FDR. At this meeting, Randolph stated that the march would be called off only if the president issued an executive order banning segregation in defense industry jobs. At one point, FDR asked Randolph how many people were expected at the march. He was stunned when Randolph told him that 100,000 marchers were ready to come. In the end, FDR agreed to what became Executive Order 8802, forbidding discrimination in industries holding government contracts for war production and in training for jobs in war industries. Executive Order 8802 was signed on June 25. As promised, Randolph called off the march.

The defense industry would soon be employing many more people. Six months after the Executive Order, on December 7, 1941,

Japanese pilots attacked Hawaii's Pearl Harbor, damaging or destroying a significant number of American ships and aircraft, wounding some 1,100 people, and killing roughly 2,200. America declared war on Japan on December 8.

On December 7, 1941, messman Dorie Miller, the twenty-two-year-old son of a Texas sharecropper, was on the burning deck of the U.S.S. *West Virginia,* one of the battleships at Pearl Harbor. After Miller carried the ship's mortally wounded captain to safety, he manned an anti-aircraft gun and brought down what witnesses said were four Japanese planes (officials listed two). Miller had never been taught to fire the anti-aircraft gun; it was against Navy regulations for blacks to do so. Only when the ammunition was exhausted and the *West Virginia* was sinking beneath him did he abandon ship. It took three months for his heroism to be officially recognized.

The first Navy dispatches from Pearl Harbor referenced Miller as an "unidentified Negro messman." When Miller's name was officially released in March, *The Pittsburgh Courier* campaigned futilely for him to receive the Medal of Honor. In May, after considerable pressure from civil rights organizations, Miller became (to the disapproval of Secretary Knox) the first black to win the Navy Cross. After Miller's heroics, Navy regulations required that all hands, including messmen and stewards, receive anti-aircraft training. But Miller died, still a messman, on Thanksgiving Day, 1943, when all hands went down on the torpedoed carrier *Liscome Bay.*

* * *

By early 1942, the Allied grand strategy was in place: to back Germany into a corner and to take back the Pacific, island by island. A great multinational army was envisioned to choke off Germany. Under British or American command, it would come from North Africa in the south, Britain in the north, and, eventually, the Soviet Union in the east. Allied forces, although fighting in national groups, were in many ways treated as a single unit. The term "United Nations" began to be used in 1942, the year that the twenty-six Allied nations pledged not to make separate peace treaties with the Axis powers, as Germany, Japan, Italy, and nations in league with them were called.

The first half of 1942 was a terrible time for the Allies. Germany controlled most of continental Europe. British and American soldiers and sailors were forced into a devastating two-thousand-mile retreat from the Philippines to Australia. Japan, which already controlled much of China, seized the Dutch East Indies, Kuala Lumpur, Burma, Singapore, Java, Rangoon, Mandalay, Corregidor, and Bataan—where, in the emergency of the Japanese invasion, elements of the black 25th Regiment fought side by side with white Marines.

In the spring of 1942, the tide began to turn. Colonel Jimmy Doolittle bombed Tokyo and other cities in Japan. The American Navy defeated Japan in the Coral Sea and at the pivotal Battle of Midway. And U.S. Marines landed on Guadalcanal, beginning the process of recapturing the Pacific islands. In Europe, Britain's RAF bombed Berlin. (By the end of 1943, there would be round-the-clock bombing of Germany.) On the eastern front, in November 1942, the Soviet Union's Red Army stopped the Germans at Stalingrad. That same month, Britain's Field Marshal Bernard Montgomery finally defeated Germany's Field Marshal

Erwin Rommel's Afrika Korps at El Alamein. Around this time, in America, the men of the 99th Pursuit Squadron, who called themselves the Lonely Eagles, were itching to get into the fight.

In January 1941, one day after a Howard University student, Yancey Williams, had threatened to sue the secretary of war to consider his Air Corps cadet-training application, the Army had announced the formation of the first black Air Corps unit, the 99th Pursuit Squadron (later Fighter Squadron). The first black Army Air Corps pilots became known as the Tuskegee Airmen because their first training center was in Tuskegee, Alabama. This new, million-dollar Tuskegee Army Air Field (TAAF) became the center of black World War II military aviation. With twenty-seven planes, thirty-three officer pilots, and four hundred enlisted technical crew, the 99th Pursuit Squadron was listed as "experimental."

Conveniently for the Army Air Corps, Captain Benjamin O. Davis, Jr., had always wanted to fly. With Davis in command of the first black squadrons, there was no need for the Army to commission another black line officer.

Born in Washington, D.C., in 1912, Benjamin Davis, Jr., had been "overwhelmed" by his first flight, which took place at a Washington air show in 1926. Charles Lindbergh's history-making nonstop flight across the Atlantic Ocean (New York to Paris) in 1927 capped young Davis's desire to fly. Years later, in October 1935, after receiving aviation training with his West Point class, Davis had applied for the Army Air Corps, but to no avail: at the time, the Army Air Corps had no plans to integrate its units nor to create black units.

Davis graduated from West Point in 1936, sixty years after the first black graduate, Lieutenant Henry Ossian Flipper. In sixty years, West Point's racial mind-set had changed little. For almost the entirety of his four years at West Point, most cadets never spoke to Davis—other than in the line of duty. Cadets refused to eat with him and sit next to him on the way to football games. "My father had taught me to be strong," Davis wrote in his autobiography, "he had endured adversity, and so could I." Letters and visits (nearly every Saturday for two years) from his girlfriend (and future wife), Agatha Scott, were of great help in enduring the adversity.

Davis could not fathom how West Point officials and cadets, "with their continually and vociferously stated belief in 'Duty, Honor, Country,'" could rationalize their treatment of him. (The future general William Westmoreland was among Davis's "silent" classmates.) Their aim was to drive Davis out of West Point, but he graduated 35th in a class of 276.

Davis was stationed at Fort Riley, Kansas, serving as his father's aide, when in early 1941 he learned that he was being transferred to what became TAAF for pilot training. (His father had been promoted to Brigadier General in 1940 and put in command of Fort Riley's 4th Cavalry, made up of the old Buffalo Soldiers regiments, the 9th and 10th Cavalries.)

On March 7, 1942, after eight months of training, Benjamin O. Davis, Jr., and Lieutenants Lemuel Custis, Charles DeBow, George "Spanky" Roberts, and Mac Ross became the first black pilots of America's Army Air Force (the name had been changed from Air Corps to Air Force in June 1941).

Every four and a half weeks, under a rigid quota system, a few new men entered pilot training. Tuskegee was soon producing more black pilots than the Air Force would allow itself to use. Three more black fighter squadrons were created—the 100th, 301st, and 302nd—which made up the 332nd Fighter Group, activated in mid-1942.

The TAAF base commander was a West Point graduate, Colonel Frederick von Kimble. When Kimble became base commander, he segregated the formerly integrated base. "For Colored Officers" and "For White Officers" signs were posted everywhere. According to Davis, Kimble also vowed that as long as he was in charge, no black officer would be promoted above the rank of captain. What's more, he refused to give high-ranking officers jobs they were capable of doing. When the black press found out about that, they began an immediate campaign for his removal.

In mid-1942, Kimble was replaced by Lieutenant Colonel Noel F. Parrish, who had studied black history and attended lectures on race relations at the University of Chicago. Parrish was "eager to understand blacks and treat them on an equal, man-to-man basis," wrote Davis, who became a lieutenant colonel in mid-May 1942, the only black Air Force officer above the rank of captain. (He would become a full colonel in 1944.)

By July 1942, the men of the 99th were, in Davis's opinion, as ready as they were "ever going to be," but there were rumors that they would never see combat. Meanwhile, antagonism between black airfield personnel and white townsfolk was reaching the boiling point.

In early 1943, when town police attempted to seize the weapons of black MPs on Tuskegee property, a riot was barely averted. Armed warfare almost broke out when an Army nurse stationed at Tuskegee, Lieutenant Nora Green, was beaten and thrown into jail for refusing to move from a "white" bus seat while traveling from the base to the town.

In March, Tuskegee's director, Frederick Patterson, turned to Eleanor Roosevelt. "Morale is disturbed by the fact that the 99th Pursuit Squadron trained for more than a year and is still at Tuskegee and virtually idle," he wrote. Mrs. Roosevelt sent Patterson's letter to Secretary of War Henry Stimson with a covering note of her own: "This seems to me a really crucial situation." In early April, the 99th was off to North Africa, where Allied forces were engaged in Operation Torch.

In late 1942, 400,000 American troops had landed in French North Africa, where all Allied armies were placed under the command of General Dwight D. Eisenhower, commander in chief of American forces in the European theater. The goal of the Allies was to control Morocco, Algeria, and Tunisia and the Mediterranean Sea, which meant breaking the hold that German and Italian forces had on territory on the Mediterranean coast between Tunis and Egypt.

The Allies were victorious in May 1943, when, on Cap Bon Peninsula, near Tunis, roughly 275,000 Axis forces surrendered. The 99th Squadron arrived in Morocco before the Axis surrender, joining the rest of the Allies in the Mediterranean theater in preparing for the Sicilian campaign, the first step in the battle for Italy. The Lonely Eagles had received brand-new P-40s to fly.

On July 2, 1943, Buster Hall, escorting B-25s over Sicily, became the first black American pilot to shoot down an enemy aircraft (in this case a Focke-Wulf 190). For this, the 99th's first kill, Hall was awarded the Distinguished Flying Cross. Hall's victory was an exception, not the rule. The 99th's short-range P-40s kept them out of the initial invasion, and they spent the rest of the Sicilian campaign out of the war zone, covering shipping and escorting bombers to Salerno.

In July 1943, an Allied force under British command landed in Sicily and captured Palermo. Benito Mussolini, the Fascist leader of Italy, was overthrown. And having secured a foothold in Italy, the Allies planned an all-out assault. The invasion of Italy, planned for September 9, called for the use of all available combat air units. The 99th was ordered to rejoin the 33rd Fighter Group, to which the squadron had been attached in North Africa.

Colonel William "Spike" Momyer, the commander of the 33rd's P-40 squadrons, made life as difficult as possible for the 99th—from giving pilots the wrong briefing times to publicly criticizing their low kill count. He then submitted a report to the Air Force stating that the 99th was "not of the fighting caliber of any squadron in this Group."

Air Force Commanding General Henry H. "Hap" Arnold recommended to Army Chief of Staff General George C. Marshall that the 99th be removed from combat and that the 332nd be sent to a noncombat area. Arnold also recommended that plans for a black bombardment group, the 477th, be scrapped.

In early September 1943, Benjamin O. Davis, Jr., was called home, officially to take command of the 332nd Fighter Group but in reality to fight for the future of blacks in the Air Force. In October, Davis appeared before a commission on the use of black troops. His spirited defense of black pilots saved the 99th for combat. What's more, the "experiment" was expanded: the 477th Bomber Group was activated.

While Davis was at home, the 99th, led by Major George Roberts, was reassigned to the 79th Fighter Group. This time around the 99th flew integrated missions and was treated like any other squadron in the group.

On November 30, 1943, the 79th Fighter Group set a record of twenty-six missions, nine of which were flown by the 99th alone. Within weeks the 99th was flying thirty-six to forty-eight sorties a day. American air action enabled Allied forces to finally establish an Italian beachhead, at Anzio—and Anzio Beach was the key to Rome.

January 27 and 28, 1944, were two of the best Allied air combat days of the entire Italian campaign. Allied bombers counted fifty kills, and Allied fighters counted eighty-five, twelve of which belonged to the 99th.

On January 27, outnumbered two to one, Captain Clarence Jamison's flight of twelve planes knocked out five German planes in less than five minutes, causing those remaining to turn and run. When they returned to their home base, each of the twelve pilots buzzed the field and made a slow victory roll. Later that day, Captain Lemuel Custis and Lieutenants Charles Bailey and Wilson Eagleson knocked out three more German planes. The next day, Lieutenants Lewis C. Smith and Robert Deiz each claimed one. And Buster Hall, owner of the first kill, knocked out two more enemy planes, winning another Distinguished Flying Cross. In the next two weeks, the 99th's kill total rose to twenty-four—a fighter-squadron record. The unit received an official commendation from the formerly antagonistic Hap Arnold.

While the 99th was winning its wings in the Mediterranean, the 332nd Fighter Group—the 100th, 301st, and 302nd squadrons— were at home with serious morale problems. In April 1943, they had been transferred from TAAF to Selfridge Field, outside Detroit. There, the base commander barred the black officers, under threat of arrest, from the officers' club—this despite War Department A-R (Army Regulation) 210-10, specifically stating that all officers' clubs were open to all officers. Detroit, scene of a race riot in June 1943, was even worse than the airfield. Black officers in downtown Detroit constantly confronted white soldiers who refused to salute.

"Didn't you see me?" Captain Lee "Buddy" Archer, with the 302nd, demanded of a nonsaluting white soldier.

"Yes," the man replied.

"Yes, what?" Archer barked.

"Yes, sir!" replied the white soldier. Indicating his girlfriend, he added, "I was gonna salute, but she held my arm."

Archer made the soldier salute, to his girlfriend's fury.

When Benjamin O. Davis, Jr., finally assumed command of the 332nd in October 1943, racial tension was near eruption. "They decided to get us overseas," Archer said. In February 1944, the 332nd arrived in Naples. Their emblem was a fire-spitting black panther over a white star.

The 332nd saw heavy action in support of Allied ground troops converging on Rome in May 1944. The city finally fell on June 4, two days before the Normandy invasion. Rome was the first Axis capital to fall, and June was a busy month: Allied strategy was to keep the enemy fully occupied in Italy.

On June 25, Captain Wendell "Hot Rock" Pruitt and Lieutenant Gwynne Peirson knocked out a German destroyer in Trieste harbor with machine guns—a feat unique in Air Force history. Pruitt hit the magazine, setting it on fire, and Peirson's strike created the explosion. Wing cameras furnished proof to the skeptical 15th Air Force. Pruitt was awarded the Air Medal with six oak-leaf clusters, and the Distinguished Flying Cross.

Hot Rock Pruitt was unofficially regarded as the best pilot in the outfit. Lee Archer flew wingman for him. "No one could beat Pruitt and myself," Archer told me. "Wendell Pruitt was probably—no, positively—the most popular pilot in the 332nd," the 332nd's intelligence officer, Major Robert Pitts, was quoted as saying in *The Invisible Soldier*. "The second man would be Lee Archer. . . . They were both top flyers, they were superb in the air, and they were veteran flyers, but both had time to talk to and give advice to a novice. They flew like birds but they kept their feet on the ground."

Archer became the first black ace. Known as the Whistler, he always whistled or sang in his plane. His confidence that he could kill, evade, and escape in the air was total. He believed that nothing could hit him from the ground.

Pruitt was more of an artist. After each mission, when all the other pilots had landed, he would entertain the ground crew. "He would circle the base, tip his wings, go into chandelle and a couple of rolls," said Robert Pitts. "After about ten or fifteen minutes of beautiful flying, he would come in for a perfect three-point landing. Any other pilot would have been chewed out by the boss." Pruitt was apparently the only pilot whom Colonel Davis could never severely reprimand. "Maybe it was because all the men on the ground and particularly his crew chief really loved the guy," said Pitts. "Everybody respected him, and he knew the guys that kept them flying would like to see a little show now and then." Pruitt died in April 1945, when he crashed in the midst of a victory roll at Tuskegee.

In April 1945, while the men of the 332nd were shooting down the last enemy aircraft over the Mediterranean, 101 black officers of the 477th Bombardment Group were shooting down military injustice at home.

The 101 pilots were arrested at Freeman Field, Indiana, for staging group sit-ins at the officers' club after Freeman Field's commander, Colonel Robert Selway, illegally barred black officers from the club. Advised by the NAACP as well as their own barracks lawyer, Lieutenant William Coleman, Jr., the men had expected arrest and pledged themselves to nonviolence. Of the 101 officers arrested, only 2 were tried, and were subsequently acquitted. A third, accused of shoving a superior officer, was charged under Article 64, which comprised military crimes punishable by death, but in the end he was merely fined $150. As a consequence of the incident, Air Force Chief Hap Arnold put Colonel Benjamin O. Davis, Jr., in command of the 477th, by then based at Godman Field, Kentucky—making Davis the first black base commander in the Air Force.

The spring of 1945 saw the final Allied assault on Germany as all fronts converged—north, south, and east. The 332nd took part in the all-out offensive against industry in the German-occupied Balkans, especially the vast and heavily defended Romanian oil fields at Ploiesti.

By late April, the 332nd had shot down 111 enemy aircraft, destroyed 150 other planes on the ground in strafing runs, and flown 1,578 combat missions, more than any other unit in Europe. Of the 450 black fighter pilots who saw combat during World War II, 65 were killed in action and 23 were shot down to become German prisoners of war. The 332nd Fighter Group won 3 Distinguished Unit Citations, 150 Distinguished Flying Crosses, a Silver Star, a Legion of Merit, 14 Bronze Stars, 744 Air Medals and Clusters, 8 Purple Hearts, and the Red Star of Yugoslavia. They were the only American fighter-escort group never to lose a bomber.

During World War II, black women did war work on several fronts, including as nurses and Red Cross workers. They also made their mark in the Women's Army Corps—the WACs (originally WAACs—Women's Army Auxiliary Corps—when established in 1942). One of the black WAC battalions was the 6888th Central Postal Directory Battalion— the "Six Triple Eight." The eight hundred women of the Six Triple Eight who served in Europe were under the command of Major Charity Adams, the first black officer in the Women's Army Corps.

Adams, a graduate of Wilberforce and a former math and science teacher, started officer candidate training at Fort Des Moines, Iowa, where living quarters were segregated but training was not. "We were thirty-nine different personalities, from different family backgrounds and different vocational experiences. . . . We were the ambitious, the patriotic, the adventurous," said Adams in her memoir, *One Woman's Army,* of the first black WAAC officers-to-be. They were married, single, divorced, engaged; college professors, housewives, and domestic workers. Graduation day was August 29, 1942. The first WAAC Officer Candidate School class of 440 women included 40 black women.

In December 1945, Adams and black WAC Captain Abbie Noel Campbell were sent to Britain to prepare for their troops, who would be responsible for redirecting mail to roughly 7 million U.S. personnel in the European theater, from uniformed military to civilian specialists and Red Cross workers. "No mail, low morale" was the battalion motto. The Six Triple Eight worked seven days a week in three eight-hour shifts.

The only fully integrated service in the World War II U.S. military was the Merchant Marines, representing the war effort of America's civilian shipping fleet. Carrying everything from troops to food to fighter planes, Merchant fleets dodged torpedoes back and forth across the Atlantic. (The Merchant Marine casualty rate was second only to that of the Marine Corps. Some five thousand seamen were killed in 1942 alone, braving the Murmansk Run to the northern Soviet Union.)

The Merchant Marines refused to wear uniforms. Their only concession to the military was a badge on their caps. Hugh Mulzac, veteran of the World War I Merchant Navy, was the first black captain in the U.S. Merchant Marines. His ship was the *Booker T. Washington.* (The *George Washington Carver,* another Merchant Marine ship, was christened by my mother in May 1943.) Officers serving under Mulzac on the *Booker T. Washington* included Joseph Williams, the first black graduate of the Merchant Marine officers academy. The oldest Merchant seaman was William Lew, a sturdy seventy-eight-year-old black man who volunteered in August 1943. Lew was the great-great-grandson of Barzillai Lew, who had served in the American Revolution.

The Navy remained the least integrated branch of America's armed forces. Things began to change after FDR gave the Navy a nudge.

Stung by a January 1942 speech in which Wendell Willkie blasted Navy racial policy as a "mockery" of democracy, FDR (once assistant secretary of the Navy) wrote to Secretary of the Navy Frank Knox: "I think that with all the Navy activities the Bureau of Navigation might invent something that colored enlistees could do in addition to the rating of messmen."

A Navy study board insisted that because of close association on board ship, "members of the colored race be accepted only in the messman branch." FDR told Knox that the report was unsatisfactory. On April 7, 1942, Knox announced that 277 black volunteers per week would be accepted for enlistment, to be trained for service in a range of positions, including as clerks, gunners, signalmen, radio operators, and ammunition handlers. They would be trained in segregated units and could rise in rank no higher than petty officer. Except as stewards and messmen, blacks were still barred from seagoing duty.

Black enlistment began on June 1, 1942, at Camp Robert Smalls (named for the black Civil War naval hero). The camp was in an isolated section of the Great Lakes Naval Training Center outside Chicago. By February 1943, under the Selective Service

Act, the Navy had a new quota of twelve hundred black sailors a month for general service, fifteen hundred for the messmen's branch. Approximately half of all blacks would be detailed to shore billets within the continental United States, and most were assigned to ammunition and supply depots. In June and July 1943, there were two serious incidents of racial unrest in the Navy, the first of many during the war: at a Virginia ammunition depot and in a construction battalion on a Caribbean transport.

Because of these incidents, a small "Special Program Unit" was created to deal with racial problems and coordinate policies for black sailors. The Special Program Unit encouraged the training of a black shore patrol (Navy police), established a training center with black faculty for illiterate draftees at Camp Robert Smalls, and got the Navy to rule that except for special units, no black sailor could be assigned to maintenance or stevedore work in the continental United States. The Unit was also responsible for two "experiments," one of which was assigning 53 black seamen and 14 white officers to the submarine chaser PC 1264.

The other experiment was the commissioning of the U.S.S. *Mason*, a destroyer escort with a crew of 196 black enlisted men and 44 white officers. The crew of the *Mason* was recognized for its heroism in battling ninety-mile-an-hour winds and forty-foot waves as an escort support ship to England in 1944. Sadly, the recognition came fifty years after the fact: a convoy commander's recommendation of letters of commendation for the *Mason* had been "lost" in official channels.

By the fall of 1943, after congressional queries and much protest from civil rights organizations, the Navy began to examine the question of black officers. At that time, there were three roads to Navy commission: the Naval Academy at Annapolis; the

Navy's V-12 Program (part of the Naval Reserve Officers Training Corps); and direct commission from enlisted ranks or civilian life.

Annapolis remained closed to blacks until 1945, and only a few black V-12 reservists had been enlisted. The first sixteen black officer candidates to begin segregated training at Great Lakes on January 1, 1944, were chosen from among top enlisted personnel. They would receive only eight weeks of training—half the normal period.

Suspecting that they were being sabotaged, the black officer candidates covered their windows with blankets after lights-out and continued studying. Their exam scores were so high that they were retested. The second results were even higher: the best class scores ever recorded at Great Lakes. The Navy decided, however, that only twelve of the sixteen would be commissioned. A thirteenth, with outstanding grades, was permitted to become a warrant officer. They were known as the Golden Thirteen, and each one of them was officially designated "Deck Officers Limited—Only." This category was usually reserved for officers whose physical or educational deficiencies kept them from performing all line-officer duties.

Frank Knox died in April 1944. He was replaced by his former undersecretary, James Forrestal. The time had come, Forrestal felt, to "expand the use of Negro personnel by assigning them to general sea duty," and he began laying plans that made this a reality.

On July 17, 1944, the Navy suffered the worst home-front disaster of the war with the explosion of two military cargo ships at

Port Chicago, California. Three hundred and twenty sailors were killed, including two hundred and two black ammunition loaders. The accident represented more than 15 percent of all black naval casualties—and the worst domestic loss of life—during World War II. Congress proposed compensation of up to $5,000 to the families of the victims, but Mississippi's Representative John Rankin objected because most of the prospective recipients were black. Maximum compensation was reduced to $3,000.

Less than a month after the explosion, 258 of the surviving black seamen, denied the thirty-day leave granted to white survivors, refused to load ammunition at a nearby port under the unsafe conditions. They were arrested. Fifty of those arrested were singled out and charged with mutiny, a crime punishable by death. All the sailors were convicted and given long prison terms. "This is not fifty men on trial for mutiny," said the NAACP lawyer Thurgood Marshall, defending the accused sailors. "This is the Navy on trial for its whole vicious policy toward Negroes." Thanks in large part to Marshall's efforts, forty-seven of the fifty protestors were released two years later.

On July 28, 1944, James Forrestal recommended that black women be accepted into the Navy's WAVES (Women Accepted for Volunteer Emergency Service). Black WAVES would be trained on an integrated basis and assigned "wherever needed within the continental limits of the United States, preferably to stations where there are already Negro men."

The integration of black women into the Navy found a strong ally in the WAVES director, Captain Mildred H. McAfee, but she could not, however, combat entrenched Navy racism. While the first Women's Auxiliary Army Corps officer candidate school class of 440 had included 40 black women, the last training class of WAVES included only 2: thirty-year-old Lieutenant, junior grade, Harriet Pickens (who was engaged to my great-uncle Sergeant John Burke Horne) and twenty-six-year-old Ensign Frances Wills. Pickens and Wills, both New Yorkers, graduated from training at Smith College on December 21, 1944. Despite the handicap of joining the class when one-third of the eight-week course was over, Pickens, daughter of NAACP official William Pickens, graduated third. She received a personal letter of congratulation from First Lady Eleanor Roosevelt—and endless GI fan mail.

An October 1944 directive ordered the Navy, the Coast Guard, and the Marines to enroll black women on a nondiscriminatory basis. The Coast Guard accepted a small number of black female enlistees, but the Marine Corps Women's Reserve did not enroll blacks until 1949.

The Marine Corps was the last of the military services to accept black volunteers. Enlistment began in June 1942. The black recruits, 75 percent of whom had some college education, included specialized technicians, teachers, ROTC grads, and even Army professionals who had relinquished their commissions for the Marine Corps. But there would be no black Marine officers, despite the superior quality of these recruits.

Montford Point Marine training center, in North Carolina, was home to the first black Marines, who began arriving there in late August 1942. Montford Point was a swampy, mosquito-ridden, snake- and bear-infested forest behind Camp Lejeune.

At Montford Point, a token two defense battalions (seacoast artillery, anti-aircraft artillery, and infantry and tank units for overseas base defense) would be trained for combat: the 51st and the 52nd Defense Battalions. The rest of the seventeen thousand black Marines were trained for the noncombat messmen and stewards branches and for depot and ammunition companies.

Depot and ammunition companies, which often served in the line of fire, hauling supplies onto beaches during offensives and guarding and delivering ammo, were trained only in the use of light firearms. From October 1943 until September 1944, one ammunition company and two depot companies were organized every month at Montford Point. The Marine Corps had discovered a useful role for the unwanted black recruits. Placing them in formerly white labor battalions as Pacific support troops would, according to Marine leadership, free more white Marines for fighting.

One of the earliest black Marine recruits was Edgar R. Huff, Jr., of Gadsden, Alabama, whose father had served in World War I (in Signal Corps Intelligence) and had died from mustard gas in France. Huff, who stood over six feet tall and weighed nearly two hundred pounds, enlisted at age twenty-two with a quarter in his pocket, a quarter he was to carry for thirty years, for good luck. "I wanted to be a Marine," Huff told the authors of *Blacks in the Marine Corps*, "because I had always heard that the Marine Corps was the toughest outfit going and I felt that I was the toughest going, and so I wanted to be a member of the best organization."

"You may as well go over the hill, or go home tonight," white drill instructors (DIs) yelled at the black recruits standing at attention in their undershorts at one A.M. on the second night of boot camp, "because you'll never make good Marines!" These recruits stood at attention for two hours, as mosquitoes attacked. When they were finally allowed to return to their huts, several began to pack.

"Unpack your bags, men!" Huff commanded. "They want us to fail." Huff urged his comrades to "hold on like a bull dog on a bone. Don't let our race down; they are depending on us to succeed. Unpack your bags and stick to it like men."

When the Marine Corps decided to develop black noncommissioned officers, the best of the best black recruits became assistant drill instructors, or "acting jacks." In January 1943, Private Edgar R. Huff, promoted to private first class (PFC), became the first black Marine NCO. A month later, Huff recommended that a fellow Alabaman, Private Gilbert "Hashmark" Johnson, also be promoted.

Johnson was thirty-seven when he arrived at Montford Point. He was so impressive in his naval uniform (officer's steward, first class), with three stripes up and three stripes down his arm (thus his nickname, Hashmark), that Huff stood at attention until Johnson said, "Son, sit down." With two years of college and sixteen years' combined service in the Army and Navy, Johnson should have been promoted faster than Huff, but was considered "outspoken." (Over time, Huff and Johnson became best friends and eventually married identical-twin sisters.)

By May 1943, black sergeants and drill instructors were in charge of all training platoons at Montford. Hashmark—by then Sergeant Johnson—was chief DI. Many recruits believed that with black NCOs, boot camp became even tougher. Johnson admitted to being something of an "ogre," but the goal—to shape in a few weeks "a type of Marine fully qualified in every respect to wear that much cherished Globe and Anchor"—was "nearly impossible." Among the men who made the grade at the "impossible" was Bill Downey, a native of Des Moines, Iowa, whose grandfather had been the first black policeman in Iowa. As Downey recalled in his book, *Uncle Sam Must Be Losing the War,* he had enlisted after reading a newspaper headline that "Marines are suffering 50 percent casualties on Guadalcanal."

Despite rumors that no black Marines would actually see combat, in mid-1943 the new commanding officer, Lieutenant Colonel Floyd A. Stephenson, recommended that the 51st become a regular heavy defense battalion. In September 1943, the 51st Defense Battalion moved out of the main Montford Point area to special quarters at Camp Knox, last used for war dog training. The quarters were badly in need of repair; nevertheless, the men of the 51st stayed motivated—they were so proud to be the only black Marine unit engaged in extensive combat training. Morale soared with the arrival of three brand-new 155mm artillery guns. They named one for Lena Horne, another for boxing heavyweight champion Joe Louis, and the third "Zombie," for a 1940s movie about voodoo sleep-walking killers.

The 51st became known as a hotshot shooting outfit. In November 1943, on the last day of gunnery training, with more military brass on the beach than ever before, the men broke all existing coastal and anti-aircraft firing records. The achievement remained a secret, but their scores shot them into the war. In January 1944, they were on their way to the Pacific.

*   *   *

"This is a troop train of the United States Marines on their way to a port of disembarkment." This from a lieutenant with the 51st to a southern sheriff who refused to let the men get off the train for food. And after making it quite clear that he didn't care where the men were headed, the sheriff said, "They ain't goin' to eat in Atlanta, Georgia, with white folks." When an officer returned with news that German POWs were eating in the station cafeteria, the men wanted to empty the train and take the station apart. "It was so frustrating that some of the guys actually wept," Downey wrote. "There was no place to hide their tears or their shame."

On February 11, 1944, the 51st sailed for Nanumea and Funafuti, two of the nine islands of the British-ruled Ellice Islands. The 51st had been sent to the Ellice Islands to relieve the white 7th Defense Battalion, and their job was to maintain and defend island airfields. The greatest dangers, the men were told, were mildew, fungus, and warts.

Six months after the 51st arrived on the Ellice Islands, they were sent to Eniwetok atoll, in the Marshall Islands. This time the 51st took over the weapons and equipment of the 10th Antiaircraft Battalion. The men of 51st sharpened their gunnery talents, and, according to the record books, they were the best gunners in the Marine Corps. But these first black combat Marines spent nineteen months in the Pacific, until the war's end, without seeing combat.

The only black Marines to see combat were not combat troops. They were members of ammunition and depot companies, who earned high praise (and citations) for their valor during battles against Japanese forces on the islands of Saipan and Guam in the summer of 1944. In September, two black Marine companies took part in the bloody battle for the island of Peleliu. Black noncombat Marines would also see action on Iwo Jima.

The 555th Parachute Infantry Battalion—the "Triple Nickels"—was America's first black paratrooper unit. Created in 1942 with all black officers, they never saw combat against Axis soldiers, but they did fight against the enemy. Sent to the Pacific Northwest in the spring of 1945 for the highly classified mission called Operation Firefly, the 555th became smoke jumpers. Operation Firefly battled forest fires created by Japanese firebombs hidden in silk and paper balloons that floated across the Pacific Ocean on the jet stream. The bombs' existence was kept secret from the public to prevent panic. The 555th conducted more than twelve hundred individual jumps, putting out fires and defusing the bombs. The hot, dry summer of 1945 saw the Triple Nickels fighting powerful Pacific Northwest forest fires, as well.

Meanwhile, in Europe, the Army was confronted with dire manpower shortages. As a consequence, yet another "experiment": black service troops were asked to volunteer for integrated combat. The call was limited to privates who had some infantry training in the upper four categories of the Army General Classification Test. Noncommissioned officers wishing to apply would have to accept a rank reduction.

A little over 2,200 black troops volunteered for combat in December 1944, to fill in for white troops killed in the ongoing Battle of the Bulge (which the Germans called the Ardennes Offensive, after the region in Belgium and Luxembourg where it took place). The black volunteers would be trained in platoons—not as "individuals." They would remain in segregated groups to which white commanders could assign white platoon sergeants and white platoon and squad leaders.

A December 1944 letter to Mississippi's notoriously racist Senator Theodore Bilbo from Robert Byrd, a future U.S. senator from West Virginia, indicated the depth of white-supremacist reaction. "Integration of the Negro into White regiments is the very thing for which the Negro intelligentsia is striving," wrote Byrd, "and such a move would serve only to lower the efficiency of the fighting units and the morale of the average white serviceman as well." Byrd also stated:

> I am a typical American, a southerner, and 27 years of age, and never in this world will I be convinced that race mixing in any field is good. All the social "do-gooders" . . . the disciples of Eleanor [Roosevelt] . . . can never alter my convictions on this question. . . . I am loyal to my country and know but reverence to her flag, BUT I shall never submit to fight beneath that banner with a negro by my side. Rather I should die a thousand times, and see old Glory trampled in the dirt never to rise again, than to see this beloved land of ours become degraded by race mongrels, a throw back to the blackest specimen from the wilds.

Unlike the black soldiers with whom he would "never submit to fight," Byrd did not serve in the military in World War II.

In late October 1944, with his Third Army bogged down in France's Saar Basin, General George S. Patton, Jr., needed replacements. The only combat armored units still in America were black.

Of three "experimental" black battalions on maneuvers in Texas, Patton chose the 761st: a 730-member battalion, with 10 white officers. This battalion's motto was "Come Out Fighting."

Patton welcomed the 761st to Normandy on November 2, 1944, in typical "Blood and Guts" style:

> *Men, you're the first Negro tankers to ever fight in the American Army. I would never have asked for you if you weren't good. I have nothing but the best in my Army. I don't care what color you are, so long as you go up there and kill those Kraut[s]. . . . Everyone has their eyes on you and is expecting great things from you. Most of all, your race is looking forward to you. Don't let them down, and, damn you, don't let me down.*

Afterward, Patton climbed aboard Private E. G. McConnell's Sherman tank to examine the new 76mm cannon. McConnell, in our 1991 interview, remembered Patton as "dapper as he could be—pearl-handled revolver and all." At age sixteen, McConnell, an ex–Boy Scout from Queens, New York, had volunteered (with parental permission) for the tank corps in 1942. A Sherman tank with a 76mm gun weighs thirty-five tons and requires a five- or six-man crew: driver, assistant driver, bow gunner, turret gunner, cannoneer, radio operator, and commander. McConnell had been trained to handle all positions.

The 761st crossed the Channel to Normandy and Omaha Beach in late October 1944, four months after D-Day, as the Allied invasion of German-held France was called. As their tanks rolled out onto shore, the 761st saw the wreckage of D-Day ships, tanks, and trucks, and of German bunkers.

The 761st had been assigned to Patton's 26th Infantry Division, commanded by Major General Willard S. Paul, 26th Infantry commander. "We have been expecting you for a long time," said Paul when he welcomed the battalion to Normandy, "and I am sure that you are going to give a good account of yourselves. I've got a big hill up there that I want you to take, and I believe that you are going to do a great job of it." November 8, 1944, found the 761st leading 26th Division infantrymen through a landscape of snow, sleet, and mud toward the town of Bezange la Petite and Hill 253 (General Paul's "big hill").

The 761st's A Company's popular young white captain, David Williams II, described himself as "a young punk out of Yale who also changed as the action went along." He knew no blacks except for the family maid and chauffeur, and considered himself a "most unlikely candidate" for black troops. "But I got my manhood with them," Williams later told *The New York Times*. "These guys were better than heroes because they weren't supposed to be able to fight, and they were treated worse than lepers. I can tell you, it took a rare sort of character to go out there and do what they did. I used to ask myself, why . . . should these guys fight? Why?"

Rolling in a mile and a half behind Williams, E. G. McConnell saw A Company "slaughtered," and white infantrymen sprawled all over the ground by the German counteroffensive. Private Clifford C. Adams, a medic from Waco, Texas, was the first of the 761st to be killed—hit by an exploding shell while rendering aid to an injured soldier.

Staff Sergeant Ruben Rivers, of Tecumseh, Oklahoma, opened the way for the capture of the town and the hill by climbing out of his tank under heavy fire to dismantle a roadblock. Rivers would be responsible for more than three hundred German deaths between the towns of Hampont and Guebling alone. "Rivers led the way!" became a byword for bravery. Whenever his company attacked, Rivers's tank was always first into a town. But Rivers met his fate at Guebling, where his head was blown off. He won a posthumous Silver Star.

As three Third Army divisions slowly encircled the town of Metz, the 26th Infantry, the Ninth Air Force, and the 761st Tankers were closing off all entrances and exits. Resistance was stiff, and every inch was contested, even as the enemy withdrew. Five out of eleven tanks were lost at Honskirch on November 25. McConnell's tank was hit several times and he was knocked out, wounded in the head and arm. Waking up in a ditch, he thought he was dead or blind: his eyes were closed by blood. V-mail wadded in his helmet probably saved his life. When medics tried to put him in a jeep, he insisted on walking. "Get the other guys," he said. Forced into the jeep, he found hundreds of moaning and crying wounded at the aid station, and a stack of bodies five feet high. After his wounds healed, McConnell, recipient of a Purple Heart, was reassigned to the quartermasters, but he demanded to return to the 761st and hitched a ride back to the front.

In early December, the 761st's B Company broke through the French Maginot Line at Aachen and Etting. On December 11, the exhausted 26th Infantry was relieved. Infantry front lines were sent back to rest every three or four weeks, but there was no rest for the 761st. "Never once," remembered E. G. McConnell in 1991, "never once a shower truck. We washed with snow. Never once a Red Cross doughnut truck." McConnell refused ever to contribute to the Red Cross because it "totally ignored" black GIs.

The unrelieved 761st and the green 87th crossed into Germany just as the order came to turn around and dash back to The Ardennes for the Battle of the Bulge. On Christmas Eve, in two to four feet of snow and ice, the 761st was streaming northward, around and above beleaguered Bastogne, joining Lieutenant General Courtney S. Hodges's First Army. The 761st encountered what was left of Germany's 13th SS Panzers.

The Germans made their toughest stand at Tillet, but after five furious days during which neither side yielded an inch, they began to retreat. The men of the 761st and the 87th had helped push German forces sixty miles back into Germany. Now they were following the Germans into their own land.

In March, joining the 103rd Infantry in Alsace-Lorraine, the 761st was ready to crack the Siegfried Line, the zone of heavy fortifications built in Germany directly in front of the Maginot Line, and make for the Rhine. They rode so far and fast along icy mountain curves that they were soon out of range of their own artillery. But the 761st and the 103rd overran retreating enemy columns. After knocking out Siegfried defenses at Reisdorf, tankers from the 761st's C Company shared celebratory fried eggs with infantrymen of the 103rd's 409th Regiment.

In the fifteen miles between Reisdorf and Klingenmunster—the latter on the far side of the mountains, beyond the Siegfried Line—C Company took out two anti-tank guns, twenty-four pillboxes, and nine machine-gun nests. They killed 265 Germans and captured 1,450. They had faced elements of fourteen different German divisions.

With white infantry riding the tanks or flanking them in the woods, the 761st set off across Germany to capture a thousand SS troops, "liberate" camera factories and a cognac factory, and find beds to sleep in for the first time in months. Two platoons of the 761st, led by Second Lieutenants Frank C. Cochrane and Moses E. Dade, took part in the fighting that led to the capture of the castle of Reich Marshal Hermann Göring, creator of the Gestapo and head of the Luftwaffe. Germans surrendered by the thousands.

Coburg fell on April 12, 1945. Two days later, after much resistance, Bayreuth fell. The German defeat was imminent. The 761st crossed the Danube River on April 27. The next morning, they were the sole armored spearhead of the assault on Regensburg, Patton's future headquarters.

The entire 761st crossed into Austria on May 4 and headed for Steyr, on the Enns River, with troops from the Soviet Union (the First Ukrainian Front) arriving on May 6. It was the great meeting of East and West, a hugely photographed and celebrated event.

The war in Europe was over.

Major General E. H. Hughes, a former personal aide to General Eisenhower, recommended the 761st for the Distinguished Unit Citation, but Eisenhower refused to sign the recommendation. In contrast, at least twelve white units to which the 761st had been attached received citations. (In 1978, after much campaigning on the part of 761st veterans, President Jimmy Carter finally signed the Distinguished Unit Citation.)

Patton had called on them in America's darkest hour. They had "come out fighting," stayed longer on the front line than any other armored battalion, and rode deeper into Germany. Between March 31 and May 6, the 761st had taken close to 107,000 prisoners, an average daily rate of about 2,800. (Their prisoners included twenty German generals.) They had also liberated the Gunskirchen concentration camp. But in the movie *Patton*

(1970), there is no mention of the 761st. Only one black person was portrayed in the film: Patton's orderly.

The end of the war in Europe was a time of great celebrations for America and her Allies. But it was also a time of mourning. FDR had died on April 12, 1945. FDR's vice president, Harry Truman, thus became president. Among the many things on his plate was the war still going on in the Pacific. The Japanese had not yet surrendered and didn't seem about to.

Back in February 1945, twenty-year-old squad leader and acting platoon sergeant Gene Doughty and the 8th Ammunition Company had been sent to Iwo Jima in the Marianas, halfway between Tokyo and U.S. Air Force bases on Saipan, the site of the largest Marine amphibious operation in the Pacific.

The 8th Ammo landed five days after the first assault wave in the face of flying bullets, shell fire, and long-range-gun fire. All they saw on the beach were dead bodies and black volcanic ash. To Doughty, it was a "hellish" landscape. Outnumbered 5th Division Marines faced intense mortar fire from enemy soldiers dug into caves with labyrinthine tunnels and underground transits. With one landing beach for armada and assault troops, the Americans were easy targets. It took Doughty forty-five minutes to dig a foxhole in the black ash, and even that did not protect from shells.

Five days after landing, Doughty and the 8th Ammo witnessed the famous moment at Iwo Jima: when six Marines from the 2nd Battalion, under heavy enemy fire, raised the American flag on Mount Suribachi, a long-inactive volcano. A mile away, the Americans on the beach applauded and cheered.

From February 19 to March 25, Marines and Japanese battled

for Iwo Jima. Black Marine service and supply troops saw more action than the white 3rd Division, waiting offshore. The "time for heroism," said Doughty, came twenty-five days after the first assault. That night, enemy combatants sprang on Doughty's unit and made for the ammunition they were guarding. The enemy came from underground, although the Marines had believed that all caves were sealed.

Some of the Japanese appeared to be unarmed; others carried spears, anything they could fight with. Korean slave laborers fought with bare hands, the Japanese having forbidden them weapons. They seemed to come wave on wave, from skirmishes to minor engagements to pocket battles. Fighting in the dark, Doughty and his men had no idea how many they were killing. At sunrise, he could not believe his eyes. His men had killed a full company or more.

Twelve black Marines were wounded and three were killed in the first month of the battle for Iwo Jima, the single fiercest contest in the Pacific. All told, more than six thousand Marines were killed and close to twenty thousand wounded, the most in a single Pacific encounter in World War II.

When the Marines left Iwo Jima, black Seabees (Navy construction crews) and the 8th Ammo stayed behind for graves registration, a function traditionally reserved for black troops. Sunday, March 3, 1945, was a day Doughty would never forget. A Navy supply ship arrived, and the men were invited on board for bacon and eggs, milk, toast, and coffee. Doughty remembered feeling "so grateful to be alive and to have fresh food." The Navy left a portable shower unit, and the Seabees rigged a hot sulfur shower from a natural underground lava spring. It was Doughty's twenty-first birthday. He felt the shower was "God's blessing."

*   *   *

The battle for Okinawa, the last Japanese island bastion, lasted from April 1 until June 21, 1945. Three black ammunition companies and four depot companies were there at the beginning. Fourteen black Marines were wounded in the campaign; one, Steward Second Class Warren N. McGrew, Jr., was killed. The island was declared secure, but there was little letup for black troops: Okinawa was to be the principal supply and staging area for the invasion of Japan. Four Marine divisions were preparing for the October 1 invasion of the Japanese mainland.

The Marines' war was brought to an end when President Truman decided that the best and quickest way to bring Japan to surrender was to drop atomic bombs on Japan. On August 6 and 9, 1945, the cities of Hiroshima and Nagasaki were, respectively, the targets of the first use of the atomic bomb. On August 14, Japan surrendered. World War II was over.

The combined efforts of black leaders, the black press, and government and military reformers ultimately brought real change in the status of blacks in the military. Between 1941 and 1945, the number of black enlisted personnel grew from 5,000 to over 1,000,000, and the number of black officers grew from 5 to over 7,000. Some 500,000 black men and women served overseas in North Africa, Europe, and the Pacific.

Three-quarters of blacks in the U.S. armed forces were in service and supply units. Although much of their duty was menial, much was also essential. Black troops built bridges, constructed airfields, drove trucks, and loaded and unloaded ships.

Black engineering and transport groups, such as the legendary Red Ball Express, built the great war highways: Burma's Stilwell Road and the Alaska Highway.

More black noncombatants had seen action than combat-trained black soldiers—and not just Marines. The 387th Separate Engineer Battalion was not a combat unit, but three of its members won Silver Stars at the Anzio beachhead, where sixty-one men had been wounded and eleven men and four officers killed. The 320th Barrage Balloon Battalion had been crucial to the initial assault at Omaha Beach during the invasion of Normandy. Huge barrage balloons, or blimps, to deter low-flying planes were installed in the third wave to prevent Luftwaffe strafing. Equally important and heroic was the 490th Port Battalion, a thousand-man unit of stevedores who had landed at Utah Beach on D-Day. For their service to assault troops, members of the 490th were awarded the Croix de Guerre and Bronze Arrowhead.

Despite all the heroism of black combat and noncombat troops, sadly, as before, black veterans came home to a country where they could be lynched for wearing a uniform. Nevertheless, when America went to war again, tens of thousands of blacks would serve in her armed forces.

KOREA

I will remember Yechon for another hundred years. Even in my nightmares I've never seen carnage, death, and destruction to equal—even to approach—that of 20 July 1950.

—Lieutenant Colonel Charles M. Bussey,
Firefight at Yechon: Courage and Racism in the Korean War

After World War II, pressure mounted for the integration of the U.S. armed forces, from both military personnel and civilians. President Harry Truman's response was to form the first presidential committee on civil rights. The committee's 1947 report, "To Secure These Rights," condemned segregation wherever it existed. This did not sit well with many whites, especially in the South, where blacks continued to be oppressed and terrorized, as happened to Macio Snipes in the summer of 1946.

"The First Nigger to Vote Will Never Vote Again," read a sign posted on a black church during the July 1946 Georgia primaries. Macio Snipes, a veteran, was the only black to vote in Taylor County, Georgia. For doing so, he was dragged from his house and shot to death. In Monroe, Georgia, two days after the election, a mob of white men forced two black veterans and their wives from a car. All four were shot, with about sixty bullets pumped into their bodies. Truman, a World War I officer, had already been sickened earlier that year by the beating and blinding in South Carolina of Sergeant Isaac Woodard, a black soldier in uniform on his way home from the Pacific.

On February 2, 1948, Truman sent the first ever Civil Rights

Message to Congress. It presented a comprehensive program, which included settlement of the claims of Japanese Americans arising out of their confinement in camps during World War II; a federal anti-lynching law; and a civil rights division in the Department of Justice. It promised to strengthen existing civil rights laws and protect everyone's right to vote. And it asked the secretary of defense to put an end to military discrimination as soon as possible. General Dwight D. Eisenhower bristled at Truman's initiatives, as did droves of Southerners, who would leave the Democratic Party for the Republican Party because of them.

On July 26, 1948, Truman issued Executive Order 9981, banning discrimination in the armed services on the basis of "race, color, religion, or national origin." Under James V. Forrestal, the Navy had declared itself integrated as early as February 1947. There was still a vast difference between Navy policy and practice, however. The majority of blacks in the Navy remained stewards and messmen.

In 1947, the Air Force had become a separate branch of the armed services, no longer part of the Army. The Air Force secretary, Stuart Symington, had long expressed the belief that segregation was wasteful and inefficient. In December 1949, the Air Force announced that integrated units, already in use, had doubled in number between June and August, with no racial conflicts.

Two years of unyielding pressure forced the Army and the Marine Corps to obey Truman's order. The President's Committee on Equality of Treatment and Opportunity in the Armed Services, under Charles Fahy, had been established in September 1948 to give the Army a push. The Fahy Committee attacked the Army's contention that segregation was neither discriminatory nor inefficient. It recommended, among other things, that all jobs be opened on the basis of qualification, without regard to race, and that the 10 percent ceiling on black enlistment be abolished. The Army finally agreed to gradual integration, starting with skilled blacks and working its way down. Enlistment quotas were finally done away with in March 1950. "Freedom to Serve," the final Fahy report on the inefficiency of segregation, was submitted to Truman on May 22 of that year.

It was around that time that the State Department received alarming, frustratingly vague information that the armed forces of "some Communist power" were expected to go into action soon, "somewhere."

Less than five years after World War II, former allies had become enemies, and former enemies had become the staunchest friends. For decades the world would be caught up in a "cold war": a struggle for power and influence between Communist nations, led by the Soviet Union, and capitalist nations, led by the United States.

In 1946, Winston Churchill announced that an "iron curtain" of Communism was descending over Eastern Europe. The Soviet Union had installed Communist governments in several countries, including Poland, Hungary, and East Germany. Three years after Churchill's "iron curtain" comment, Communist forces under the leadership of Mao Tse-tung defeated the forces of Nationalist leader Chiang Kai-shek. With Mao Tse-tung as chairman and Chou En-lai, founder of the Chinese Communist party, as premier, mainland China became the People's Republic of China. Chiang Kai-shek and his supporters fled to the island of Taiwan and established the Republic of China.

Korea had also undergone major change. In 1948, the territory north of the 38th Parallel became the Communist-led

People's Republic of Korea. Territory south of the 38th Parallel became the Republic of Korea. Peace between the two Koreas was short-lived. On June 25, 1950, North Korean troops crossed the 38th Parallel and took the city of Seoul, the capital of South Korea. The next day an emergency session of the United Nations Security Council approved the American resolution calling the invasion a breach of world peace. The resolution called on member nations to come to South Korea's aid.

On June 27, President Truman ordered U.S. air support for South Korean ground forces. He also sent naval forces to the Strait of Taiwan as a show of strength to deter mainland China from involvement. Intent on avoiding a conflict with the Soviet Union and China, America's aim was only to restore the 38th Parallel. Truman believed Korea had to be a "limited war" to prevent a third world war.

Overwhelmingly led by the United States, opposition to North Korea was officially a coalition of more than a dozen member nations of the United Nations, a few of which contributed medical contingents only. When it came to troops, eight Republic of Korea (ROK) divisions, seven U.S. divisions (as well as airpower), and one division from the British Commonwealth (comprising troops from the United Kingdom, Canada, Australia, and New Zealand) were joined by Belgian, Colombian, Greek, Dutch, and Filipino battalions, and a Turkish brigade.

From his headquarters in Tokyo, General Douglas MacArthur initially called the North Korean invasion a "mere border incident," one that would soon blow over. By June 29, however, he had concluded that even with U.S. air support, ROK troops would never push the North Korean People's Army (NKPA) back across the 38th Parallel.

Given full command over all military operations in Korea on July 2, MacArthur asked for ground troops. Rejecting Taiwan's offer of troops because he thought mainland China would feel threatened if he used them, Truman authorized the use of two American occupation divisions from Japan. He insisted, to MacArthur's extreme disapproval, that U.S. planes and vessels not be sent north of the 38th Parallel.

At first, most of the American military agreed with MacArthur that the invasion was only an "incident"—at most, a prelude to a very short war. But the combination of overwhelming North Korean manpower—in some places it outnumbered the opposition by as much as twenty to one—and Soviet tanks drove South Korean and U.N. troops back to a tiny perimeter around the port of Pusan, at the southern end of the peninsula. The Allies retreated to Pusan in raging monsoons, hundred-degree-plus temperatures, and equally raging dysentery in the ranks. It was a catastrophe. Casualties were as high as 30 percent. U.S. and ROK forces "had no tanks, no artillery, or any weapons capable of slowing the Russian tanks," wrote David McCullough in *Truman*. "World War II bazookas bounced off the Russian tanks like stones."

As of June 1950, the Eighth Army in Japan had not yet begun to desegregate—and Eighth Army racism started at the top, with General MacArthur's chief of staff, Major General Edward M. Almond. In his book *The Forgotten War* Clay Blair described Almond as "a devout anti-black bigot." Almond would act out his racism in Korea, resegregating successfully integrated units and refusing to approve medals for black soldiers.

"Ned Almond wanted the blacks out of sight and in one place." This, according to Blair, was why the 24th Infantry, part of the 25th Division's Japanese occupation force since 1945, had been sent to Gifu, halfway between Tokyo and Kobe. (In 1948, the 24th had been assigned to provide security for Kobe Base.)

The four-thousand-man 24th Infantry was the last officially designated all-black active-duty regiment in the U.S. Army. And these so-called combat troops trained only half a day, with poorly maintained war-surplus weapons, and never at night or in winter conditions.

Although the 24th Infantry had many black officers (mostly because they had few other places to go), they never commanded or supervised white officers. Black lieutenants and captains led only at platoon and company levels, while whites held field-grade positions of major and above. Most black majors were still chaplains or headquarters staff. Blacks in command positions remained rare.

With few exceptions, black officers ranked the white senior officers in the regiment as being of very low caliber. Black officers believed that white officers tolerated weaknesses in black troops that would be penalized among whites, simply because blacks were not expected to do any better. Most black officers were aware of the regiment's shortcomings, none more so than Lieutenant Colonel Forest Lofton, the 24th's highest-ranking black officer and one of the few black field-grade officers in the Army. When Lofton found out that the 24th was about to be committed to combat, he told the regiment's commander that "he wanted no part of that." The regiment was neither trained nor prepared for war, Lofton said, and he requested reassignment. Lofton remained at Gifu as commander of the detachment that maintained the base when in early July 1950, the 24th, accompanied by three other black combat units—the 159th Field Artillery Battalion, the 77th Engineer Combat Company, and the 512th Military Police Company—was rushed to Korea, along with two companies of the white 1st Battalion, 21st Infantry.

Counting on a quick victory, these troops expected to be back in Japan within a few weeks. They would be sorely disappointed. Most American soldiers saw extended, nearly unrelieved, front-line service from July 1950 to October 1951, in temperatures ranging from hundred-plus degrees to twenty below zero, in the same summer uniforms.

Despite poor equipment, Soviet tanks, and the fierceness of the NKPA, both the first American ground victory and the war's first Medal of Honor were won by 24th Infantry troopers.

One man many believed merited a Medal of Honor was commander of the 77th Engineer Combat Company, Captain Charles Bussey. One of World War II's Tuskegee Airmen and the son of a World War I veteran, Bussey joined the 25th Division in Japan in January 1950. He had rejoined the Army two years earlier, hoping to be transferred to the Air Force. Six months after Bussey joined the 25th Division, he was in the controversial Battle of Yechon.

On July 20, 1950, ten days after landing at Pusan, the 24th Infantry, the 159th Field Artillery, and Bussey's 77th Engineers were ordered to recapture the town of Yechon, north of Pusan on the Naktong River in South Korea. The sixteen-hour battle was the first combat assignment ever for most of the 24th.

With light American casualties, the 24th fought off NKPA

troops, holding the town until ROK troops could take control. In a widely publicized dispatch, Tom Lambert, the Associated Press correspondent who accompanied the 24th to Yechon, called it "the first sizable American ground victory in the Korean War." Yechon and the black regiments were hailed in newspapers around the country and in the *Congressional Record:* "First United States Victory in Korea Won by Negro GIs."

Despite being poorly trained and ill-prepared, the 24th had proved at Yechon that they could fight. As the war became a matter of swiftly shifting victory and defeat, the battle's importance faded. What's more, its existence would be doubted. In his official Army history of the first six months of the Korean War, Roy Appleman dismissed the idea that a battle had even taken place at Yechon. Veterans believed that the 24th's victory at Yechon was denied because the Army did not want its first Korean War heroes to be black. "I was there, and it was a battle as far as I was concerned, and it was a victory, too," Charles Bussey maintained in his book, *Firefight at Yechon.*

There was no question about Yechon in the mind of Major General William Kean, commander of the 25th Division. Kean gave Bussey a Purple Heart and a Silver Star for "killing a number of North Koreans." He told Bussey to regard the Silver Star as a "down payment" on a Medal of Honor. It would have made him the first black officer (though not the first black soldier) in American history to receive that honor. General Kean's recommendation never made it past General Almond's headquarters.

A month after Yechon, black soldiers' courage was again tested, and again disputed.

Late on the night of August 31, 1950, during the height of the North Korean offensive, the attacking NKPA forced the 24th Infantry to withdraw from Hill 625. Known as "Battle Mountain," Hill 625 was on the southern tip of the Pusan perimeter.

Army records state that even before the North Koreans opened fire, the 24th was seized with "mass hysteria" and ran at the first sight of the enemy, repeatedly defying white superiors' orders to stand and fight. "Two battalions [of the 24th] evaporated in the face of the enemy, and a large part of them repeated this performance four nights later," wrote Roy Appleman. The 24th was called the Bugout Brigade and the Runnin' 24th by sister units as well as by the press.

Those who had been at Battle Mountain fiercely contested the accusations of cowardice. "My company didn't disappear," said a company commander, Roger Walden, in a 1989 interview in *The Los Angeles Times.* "We were up there all night long, fighting." Walden disputed Appleman's "bug-out" account. "The North Koreans pushed through with so much force it just disrupted everything, but I saw no one break and run," Walden added. Out of about 130 men, Walden's company suffered 50 casualties.

"The regimental commander led them out," stated Charles Bussey in his defense of the 24th. "His battalion commanders were all with him. It was not a matter of the troops breaking and running. They went out under leadership. And they went back and retook it the next day." Bussey also pointed out that "the 24th Infantry Regiment lost and regained that hill for nearly forty-five days," during which time "they had no baths, very little drinking water, and seldom did they have clean clothes. Sunset provided the only respite from the hellfire of the sun." Bussey would be discharged from the Army because of illness in 1951. By then, in addition to a Purple Heart and a Silver Star, Bussey had received the Legion of Merit, the Bronze Star, the Air Medal, and the Army Commendation Medal. The Army denied that he had ever been recommended for a Medal of Honor.

Battle Mountain was one of a succession of defeats in late August and early September. These defeats led General MacArthur to go public with his quarrels with President Truman for rejecting Taiwanese troops and for keeping him out of North Korea. Then, on September 15, 1950, MacArthur roundly won the public relations battle and cemented his image as a military hero with the spectacular landing at Inchon, behind enemy lines.

Directing the action from Tokyo, MacArthur sent Marines from the Korea Strait to an amazing Yellow Sea amphibious landing at Inchon, just southwest of Seoul. It was a feat possible only two days a month because of tides.

At Inchon, North Koreans suffered some thirty thousand to forty thousand casualties. U.S. casualties were roughly 500 dead, 2,500 wounded, with 65 missing. The tide of war had turned. Victory seemed at last within reach.

When the direction of the war changed, America's attitude changed with it. Instead of merely restoring the 38th Parallel, the new military mission was to reunite Korea under the American-dominated South Korean leader, Syngman Rhee. President Truman and General MacArthur, who agreed on very little, did agree on this. However, Truman again established restrictions: U.S. planes could bomb the North, but there was to be no air or naval action against China. Furthermore, only South Korean troops could cross the 38th Parallel to fight near the Chinese border at the Yalu River. To make sure that MacArthur understood his limits, on October 15 Truman flew seven thousand miles to Wake Island in the Pacific to reiterate them. In response to Truman's concern that China might enter the war, MacArthur firmly assured the president that China would never intervene on behalf of North Korea.

By mid-October, North Korean forces had been expelled from the South, and U.N. troops had invaded the North. Troops of the American 25th Division—including the 24th Infantry, the 77th Engineers, and the 159th Field Artillery—were exactly where Truman had ordered them not to be: above the 38th Parallel, facing the Yalu River and China. They were seeking out substantial outposts of resistance near the border between North Korea and China, along the Chongchon River. They were in for a Thanksgiving surprise.

On November 23, while making its way to the Yalu River, the 25th Division was alerted that at least two Chinese divisions and part of a North Korean division were directly in front of them and heading their way. Intelligence estimates were that they faced a combined enemy force of about 34,000 men. Fervent, dedicated Communist Chinese troops had already crossed the Yalu River, attacking in strength along the Chongchon River, disconcerting the stunned U.S. troops by screaming and blowing bugles as they attacked. Within forty-eight hours of the initial onslaught, about a thousand U.S. troops were killed or wounded.

Among the American casualties was one of the few black officers awarded the Distinguished Service Cross in the Korean War. He was First Lieutenant Ellison C. Wynn, of the 9th Infantry, the first integrated regiment in Korea. When the Chinese crossed the Yalu River, the 9th was badly hit. Owing to a shortage of replacements and a liberal commanding officer, about half of the 129 men of the 9th's B Company were black. On the night of November 25, that officer, William C. Wallace, was seriously wounded. This put his executive officer, Wynn, in command.

Fierce fighting continued throughout the night. When the battle ended, Wynn was left with only thirty-four soldiers in his company. When the ammunition ran out, he began throwing rocks and canned C rations at the enemy until a grenade blew away part of his face and he finally staggered to the rear.

After the Thanksgiving surprise, American forces began what would be the largest retreat in U.S. Army history. On November 27, MacArthur, who had been urging the men to fight on, sent a cable to Washington: "We face an entirely new war." As U.S. forces withdrew, Chinese soldiers, essentially having taken over the North Korean army, broke through the 38th Parallel to claim Seoul.

The war entered a decidedly different phase after the Thanksgiving Surprise. MacArthur demanded vengeance for the sneak attack, even requesting nuclear weapons and permission to bomb and blockade China.

When the Chinese entered the war in November, Soviet-made MiGs (fighter jets) came with them. Although outnumbered five to one by MiGs, the Air Force, turning to jets, won nine out of ten dogfights.

With ground troops initially in disarray, the Air Force had many of the first early Korean victories. "Air power was the decisive factor in the Korean War," wrote World War II veteran Tuskegee airman General Benjamin O. Davis, Jr., in his autobiography. "It was air power that blunted the first North Korean attacks in the early days and later prevented the expulsion of the United Nations forces." Daniel "Chappie" James, Jr., was one of the new "fighter jocks" who switched from World War II–vintage P-51 Mustangs to jets in mid-war.

James grew up near the Pensacola, Florida, Naval Air Base and had always wanted to fly. Pilots used to take him up in return for odd jobs. Later, he became a civilian pilot teacher while waiting to make the Air Force Tuskegee quota. He eventually became a member of the all-black 477th Bombardment Group led by General Benjamin Davis, Jr. The 477th was activated in January 1944 but, owing to foot-dragging on black bomber training, had remained in America throughout World War II.

By the end of World War II, with Air Force integration under way, James had made it his goal to "get with an integrated outfit and prove that I was one of the best fighter pilots around." In September 1949, he got his chance with the 12th Fighter-Bomber Squadron at Clark Field, in the Philippines.

Early on at Clark Field, James and his family faced intense hostility from white pilots (and their wives). But he ranked first in rocketry, second in bombing accuracy, and was one of the top ground gunners in the group, as well as a basketball and baseball star. His fighter-pilot skills and confident, jovial personality eventually won the squadron over. In the spring of 1950, James won the Distinguished Service Medal when, suffering from severe burns and fractured vertebrae, he pulled a fellow pilot from a runway jet crash. After months of hospitalization, he rejoined his squadron in Korea in August 1950.

In Korea, James flew eight missions a day. He had a black panther painted on his flight helmet, his call sign was Black

Leader, and his integrated flight team was called Black Flight. James's job was to provide tactical support for ground crews, strafing at treetop level so as to destroy trains, enemy supply lines, and Soviet T-34 tanks.

In October 1950, James was flying in close support of ground forces in Namchonjom, North Korea, attacking only a few yards in front of friendly troops. Calling strike after strike until all ammunition was spent, he was responsible for over one hundred North Korean dead. After the battle, he was awarded the Distinguished Flying Cross and was promoted to captain. In late December 1950, having completed one hundred combat missions, James was sent back to the Philippines to train pilots on their way to war. By 1952 he was a major. A year later he became the first black Air Force officer commanding an integrated fighter squadron in the continental United States. James would also serve in the war in Vietnam and become, in 1975, America's first black four-star general.

While American soldiers were fighting a segregated war in Korea, integrated training began at home. Back in August 1950, two months after war was declared, the post commander of the Army training center at Fort Jackson, South Carolina, had found that he had so many recruits that it was "totally impractical to sort them out" in terms of race. He began integrated training strictly on his own. It worked so well that the Army made Fort Jackson a model. Black soldiers were assigned wherever they were needed. Fears of conflict between black and white troops proved groundless. Integrated units achieved high performance ratings. By September, the Army was finally ready for integration.

MacArthur had started his own investigation on the issue of

integration, but he was dismissed before the investigation was completed. Publicly contradicting Truman yet again, on March 20, 1951, MacArthur wrote to the Republican leader of the House of Representatives, urging the use of Taiwanese forces. On April 11, Truman dismissed MacArthur as supreme commander of the U.N. forces in Korea. His replacement was General Matthew B. Ridgway.

General Ridgway believed that segregation was not only "un-American and un-Christian" but "inefficient" and "improper." In the spring of 1951, he formally asked permission to integrate forces in Korea. On July 26, 1951, the Army announced that integration would be completed in about six months in Japan, Korea, and Okinawa—and that the all-black 24th Infantry would be disbanded.

Seoul changed hands four times during the war. As victories and defeats moved back and forth, so did peace talks.

General Dwight Eisenhower became president in January 1953 with a clear mandate to end the war, as he had promised to do during the campaign. The new secretary of state, John Foster Dulles, threatened to use both Taiwanese troops and nuclear weapons if North Korea did not go to the peace table.

On March 5, the head of the Soviet Union, Joseph Stalin, died, and the Soviet attitude changed completely. By March 10, Stalin's successor, Georgi M. Malenkov, proposed an exchange of wounded and sick prisoners of war: Malenkov hoped that this would "lead to a smooth settlement of the entire question of prisoners of war, thereby achieving an armistice in Korea, for which people throughout the world are longing."

Similar messages came from North Korea and Communist China. Although fighting continued along the truce line, peace talks resumed at Panmunjon in late May. President Syngman Rhee was the only barrier to peace. Rhee declared that South Korea would permit no concessions at all to the North. Moreover, he demanded a united country under the South. A humiliating ROK defeat, combined with threats and promises from the U.S. government, finally brought Rhee into line. The Korean armistice was signed on July 27, 1953, and sent North Korea back to the 38th Parallel, approximately where it had been when the war began.

In three years of this "limited war," some 3 million people died on both sides. Almost 2 million were Korean civilians. About 900,000 Chinese troops died, as did some 37,000 Americans.

Korea saw the birth of a new American military, integrated (more or less) from top to bottom. Both the Jim Crow Army and Jim Crow society were coming to an end. Unfortunately, the Cold War was not. If Korea was the new military's difficult birth, then Vietnam would be its stormy adolescence.

VIETNAM

They did what they thought their country needed them to do.

—Lieutenant Colonel George Forrest (retired),
speaking with the author about GIs in Vietnam

America's involvement in Vietnam began in July 1941, when Japan seized Vietnam, Cambodia, and Laos, the countries that made up French Indochina. President Franklin Roosevelt saw Japan's occupation as a threat to the U.S. rubber supply, so he froze Japanese assets in America—a major step toward the attack on Pearl Harbor.

After World War II, America supported France when it sought to restore its hold over Indochina. The French met with resistance from the Vietnamese guerilla forces of Ho Chi Minh, leader of the Vietnamese independence movement, which became known as the Vietminh. Ho Chi Minh had also formed what became known as the Vietnamese Communist Party.

By 1951, there was full-fledged war in Indochina. By 1952, the Vietminh were everywhere, and receiving arms and matériel from the Soviet Union. In September 1953, President Dwight D. Eisenhower sent a thirty-five-member military and economic mission to Saigon as the possibility of a Communist victory grew. Most Americans thought the war was purely a French affair, even though between 1950 and 1954 their nation paid for 80 percent of it—some \$2 billion.

*   *   *

On May 7, 1954, the French outpost at Dienbienphu, in an isolated valley near the Laotian border of Vietnam, fell to the Vietminh after a fifty-six-day siege. The debacle at Dienbienphu ended nearly a century of colonial rule.

Ten days after the fall of Dienbienphu, the U.S. Supreme Court ruled unanimously in *Brown v. Board of Education* that segregated schools were unconstitutional and "inherently unequal." The *Brown* case, which resulted in the outlawing of segregation in public schools, was the culmination of over twenty years of effort by the NAACP Legal Defense team. The effort had been masterminded by the lawyer Charles Hamilton Houston and followed through by his protégé, Thurgood Marshall, the lead lawyer for *Brown.*

As America's involvement in Vietnam intensified, so did the civil rights movement, with so many epic moments, including the 1955–1956 bus boycott in Montgomery, Alabama, inspired by Rosa Parks and led by Reverend Martin Luther King, Jr.; the sit-ins of the early 1960s; and the massive boycotts and marches against Jim Crow in Birmingham, Alabama, in the spring of 1963, in which hundreds of protestors, including King, were arrested. That May, in protest of racial injustice, thousands of children, including six-year-olds, faced police dogs and water cannons. In August came the great March on Washington for Jobs and Freedom, where King electrified the world with his "I Have a Dream" speech.

Among the many other events of the civil rights movement was Bloody Sunday, as March 7, 1965, came to be known: the day that demonstrators in Alabama, led by King, set out on a march from Selma to Montgomery, the state capital, to confront Governor George Wallace about the various ways blacks were prevented from exercising their right to vote. The marchers never made it to Montgomery that day: they were brutally beaten back at Selma's Edmund Pettus Bridge by mounted state troopers.

Throughout the civil rights campaign, die-hard segregationists heaped violence upon a great many soldiers in the battle for racial justice and equal opportunity. Many civil rights workers did not live to see the changes their bravery compelled their government to make, such as the Civil Rights Act of 1964 and the Voting Rights Act of 1965. All the while, the U.S. military had been a step ahead of the rest of society and was becoming a model of racial integration. The post-Korea military became an attractive career prospect for young black men, many of whom would eventually find themselves in Vietnam.

Under the terms of the Geneva agreement of July 22, 1954, Vietnam was temporarily split at the 17th Parallel, with Hanoi the capital in the North and Saigon the capital in the South. The agreement called for elections in July 1956 for a leader of a single, unified Vietnam.

The U.S. government did not look forward to the 1956 election in Vietnam. President Eisenhower observed that if an election took place, Ho Chi Minh, head of North Vietnam, would certainly win by a landslide. There was no doubt that Ho Chi Minh had more charisma than the anti-Communist man the U.S. government had chosen to back (with both money and matériel) as the head of South Vietnam: Ngo Dinh Diem. He and his family were Roman Catholics—a minority in Buddhist Vietnam, but under the French a favored and powerful minority.

Diem's close American adviser, Air Force general Edward G.

Lansdale, helped orchestrate Operation Exodus in the summer and autumn of 1954, in which nearly a million people were relocated from the North to the South. Two-thirds of them were Catholic. In the South, they provided an instant and powerful bloc of political support for Diem.

Once Diem established his authority, he set about rounding up Vietminh, who were still numerous in the South, as well as ordinary citizens who had supported the Vietminh. Eventually, while American propaganda portrayed Diem as a champion of democracy, his security forces imprisoned, tortured, and killed Vietnamese by the thousands.

In January 1955, the United States established the Military Assistance and Advisory Group (MAAG) in Saigon, and American advisers began training a South Vietnamese army. By July 1955, Diem was confident enough to denounce the Geneva agreements and declare that he would not cooperate with the scheduled elections. In October, he declared himself president of the Republic of Vietnam.

In 1957, a low-level guerrilla war ignited in the South as former Vietminh guerrillas and others antagonized and threatened by Diem's repression took up arms against his regime. Between 1957 and 1960, guerrilla forces expanded from two thousand to ten thousand. Each year, they captured thousands of weapons from the Saigon forces. Ngo Dinh Diem grew even more repressive and shrugged off American suggestions that he change his policies.

On July 8, 1959, at Bien Hoa, guerrillas killed Major Dale Buis and Sergeant Chester Ovnand, two of the fewer than five hundred American advisers in Vietnam at the time. Eventually, the names of more than 58,000 Americans would appear on the

Vietnam Memorial in Washington, D.C., as a result of the war in which U.S. armed forces and South Vietnam's Army of the Republic of Vietnam (ARVN) battled the North Vietnamese Army (NVA) and the guerilla warriors in South Vietnam, known as the Vietcong, or simply, the VC.

In February 1954, three months before Ho Chi Minh's victory at Dienbienphu and the *Brown* decision, sixteen-year-old Colin Powell registered for his first semester at City College of New York. After a brief interest in the School of Engineering, he changed his major to geology.

Geology aside, Colin Powell's real major, in which he always received A's, was the Reserve Officer Training Corps—and especially the elite "Pershing Rifles" ROTC fraternity. "The discipline, the structure, the camaraderie, the sense of belonging were what I craved," Powell wrote in his autobiography, *My American Journey*. Powell became cadet colonel—the highest ROTC rank—and Distinguished Military Graduate.

Powell's father had not been happy in 1957 to see him go to ROTC summer camp at Fort Bragg, North Carolina. Powell Senior was nervous about the South. Racial violence had erupted in Alabama in January after the Supreme Court's decision that supported the Montgomery bus boycott. Bombs had exploded in four black churches and in the homes of ministers. Willie Edwards, Jr., a black Montgomery man, had been lynched.

Powell, warned by his father not to stray from the base, was named Best Cadet, Company D, and was second-best cadet for the entire camp. He felt "marvelous" about the latter honor until a white sergeant told him why he was not number one: "You think these Southern ROTC instructors are going to go back to their colleges and say the best kid here was a Negro?"

"They have shown that the new way for Americans to stand up for their rights is to sit down." These words were uttered by Democratic presidential candidate John F. Kennedy in the spring of 1960, in the wake of some seventy thousand young people in more than a hundred southern cities having engaged in sit-ins in protest of blacks being banned from eating at lunch counters in Woolworth's and other establishments.

The election of John F. Kennedy to the presidency in 1960 was a victory for millions of progressive Americans who wanted the nation to live up to its ideals. From the start, Kennedy, commonly referred to as JFK, showed his concern about the lack of equal opportunity for blacks in America. A combat-wounded World War II veteran, JFK questioned aloud during his inaugural parade why there were so few black faces among the Coast Guard.

JFK appointed a number of blacks to high-level posts. Among them was Thurgood Marshall, who became a federal judge (and who would eventually become the first black justice on the U.S. Supreme Court). Robert Weaver, whom JFK appointed administrator of the Federal Housing and Home Finance Agency, became, at that point, the highest-ranking black government official in history.

Like President Truman, JFK bypassed Congress and made full use of his executive powers in the civil rights area. He first used the words "affirmative action" in his 1961 executive order on Title VII of the Civil Rights Act of 1960, referring to possible remedies for unlawful discrimination in employment. An executive order that same year created the President's Committee on Equal Employment Opportunity. A 1962 order forbade racial or religious discrimination in federally financed housing. JFK talked about making the world safe for "democracy, diversity and personal distinction."

In 1962, Kennedy's Committee on Equal Opportunity in the Armed Forces, the Gesell Committee, extended the military desegregation process. The committee's directive, issued by Secretary of Defense Robert McNamara, stated that military commanders must oppose discriminatory practices affecting military personnel and their dependents—both on and off base. Individual racism and racist commanders continued to exist, but openly racist attitudes were what might be called distinctly non-career-enhancing. Black servicemen found new opportunities in promotions, service schools, and civilian communities.

By late summer of 1962, Colin Powell, by then a lieutenant, had married Alma Johnson, a native of Birmingham, Alabama, and was enrolled in the Military Assistance Training Advisor course at Fort Bragg's Unconventional Warfare Center. That fall, Powell received early promotion to captain.

The adviser course finished in December 1962. The Powells left for Birmingham, where Alma would live while Colin was overseas. Two days before Christmas, Powell left for Vietnam, where Vietcong were becoming more successful every day as Diem's inept and corrupt army surrendered more weapons and territory.

Back in February 1962, the U.S. Military Assistance Command in Vietnam (MACV, pronounced "Mac-Vee") had been established in Saigon. In April, the Pentagon verified that

U.S. pilots were flying combat missions and that U.S. soldiers were actually fighting Vietcong. In December 1960, there were approximately eight hundred U.S. military personnel in Vietnam. By December 1962, there were 11,300.

A few days after Christmas, 1962, Captain Colin Powell headed north to the tropical forests of the A Shau Valley, along the Laotian border, as field adviser to a four-hundred-man infantry battalion of the ARVN. Most of the critical fighting at the time was far from the A Shau, in the Mekong Delta. Powell's base was remote and isolated, near the primitive beginnings of the Ho Chi Minh Trail, a series of jungle trails into South Vietnam from Laos and Cambodia.

Operation Grasshopper was Powell's first mission. The battalion moved out in the predawn of February 7, 1963. "Soon the long green line of troops was swallowed up by the dark jungle," he wrote. Every day in the thick tropical forest was an endless obstacle course. The Vietcong's trails were sown with punji sticks (bamboo stakes smeared with buffalo dung, to cause pain and infection). The mile-long single column of ARVN soldiers was an obvious tactical mistake, but the ARVN officers politely ignored Powell's advice for three or four parallel columns. On the sixth day of the march, Powell heard his first incoming fire. The Vietcong had attacked, killing one man and wounding another before quickly disappearing.

Powell always carried a pencil and a GI-issue pocket notebook, as he had been taught to do at Fort Benning. Typical entry: "10 Feb.: Rain. Located evacuated village; destroyed houses and 100 K [kilos] rice, 20 K corn." Ronson and Zippo lighters were used to burn houses and crops. The peasants would lose more crops as helicopters dosed them with herbicide.

During an operation near the Laotian border in July, Powell stepped on a punji stick and was briefly hospitalized. He had only four months left in-country, so his field duties were over. Back at 1st ARVN Division headquarters, he was not happy with what he saw in the upper ranks of the South Vietnamese military. "Incompetence, corruption and flashy uniforms" were the norm. "Were these the people," Powell wondered, "for whom ARVN grunts were dying in the A Shau Valley?"

"The corner has definitely been turned toward victory in Vietnam," said the U.S. Defense Department in May 1963.

"South Vietnam is on its way to victory over communist guerillas," said American ambassador Frederick Nolting, Jr., in June.

"I can safely say the end of the war is in sight," said General Paul Harkins, head of MACV.

Journalists covered the disasters of the war close-up and also reported the views of candid military advisers, who contradicted the official, cheerful assessments. Journalists who reported the contradictions often found themselves attacked by the military. "Why don't you get on the team?" Admiral Harry Felt demanded of an Associated Press reporter.

Colin Powell's assignment after Vietnam was Fort Benning's Infantry Officers Advanced Course. On November 1, 1963, he was in Saigon, ready to head home. Driving to the airport to ship his gear, he suddenly found himself in the midst of a coup. That day, the Diem government was overthrown by a group of officers led by General Duong Van Minh. The next day, November 2, Diem and his brother and chief adviser were murdered.

Powell left Vietnam shortly after the coup. On November 22, he was in an airport in Nashville, Tennessee, waiting for a flight to Birmingham, when he suddenly saw people clustered around a television set. JFK had been assassinated in Dallas while campaigning for reelection.

"Three weeks before, I had been in Vietnam on the day that that country's president had been assassinated," Powell wrote. "This afternoon, the President of my country had been murdered. And while I had been off fighting for the freedom of foreigners, four little black girls had been killed by a bomb planted in Birmingham's 16th Street Baptist Church. I had returned home, it seemed, to a world turned upside down."

In 1964, the man who had been JFK's vice president, Lyndon B. Johnson (LBJ), had no doubts about the seriousness of the problem in Vietnam that was his, now that he was president. From the start, his Vietnam policy was to prevent a Communist takeover by increasing U.S. military participation and a variety of covert programs, including harassment attacks on North Vietnam. LBJ named as the new commander of MACV General William C. Westmoreland (West Point, 1936—the class that "silenced" Benjamin O. Davis, Jr.). It was also in 1964 that South Korea got a new "commander." In January, General Nguyen Khanh ousted the original coup makers with a coup of his own.

Through the winter and spring, the Vietcong continued to seize weapons and expand the areas they controlled. The prospect that North Vietnam would take over South Vietnam grew.

During the 1964 presidential election campaign, LBJ criticized the bellicosity of his Republican rival, Senator Barry Goldwater, even as he and his advisers increased U.S. involvement in covert operations. In public, LBJ was adamant that there be no big American war in Vietnam. By June 1964, Pentagon officers were drawing up plans to bomb North Vietnam. In July, South Vietnamese commandos began a program of covert harassment attacks along the coast of North Vietnam. Then, on August 2, 1964, North Vietnamese patrol boats attacked a U.S. Navy destroyer in the Gulf of Tonkin in the vicinity of the covert operations. Two days later, a second incident was reported, but, as became clear over time, it probably never happened.

LBJ seized on the opportunity, condemned (and exaggerated) the incidents, and did not mention the covert, U.S.-backed operations against the North Vietnamese coast that had probably provoked the August 2 attack.

On August 5, LBJ ordered bombers to attack an oil depot and other installations in North Vietnam. He also managed to push the Gulf of Tonkin Resolution through Congress. The Resolution authorized him "to take all necessary measures," including the use of force, to assist any member or protocol state of the Southeast Asia Collective Defense Treaty requesting assistance in defense of its freedom. It was the equivalent of a declaration of war against North Vietnam.

After his landslide election in November 1964, LBJ began plans to send U.S. combat troops to Vietnam. In the winter of 1965, bombing was renewed in the North, and Marines, the first U.S. combat troops, landed in Danang.

* * *

Colin Powell had completed the Infantry Officers Advanced Course in May 1965. His next assignment was to teach in the school from which he had just graduated. He was also promoted to major—in less than eight years, rather than the normal ten to eleven.

To be an instructor in the Infantry Officers Advanced Course was "an impressive career credential," wrote Powell. And at the time, instructors were especially vital. "When I left Southeast Asia," Powell recalled, "it had still been a Vietnamese conflict involving some 16,000 American advisors. By the time I was asked to join the Infantry School faculty, the American involvement had begun to approach 300,000 troops, and the Army needed to produce more officers." And what an Army it was— a model of integration and high morale, with little racial tensions. Participants in the first integrated-at-the-outset American war since the Revolution stood in stark contrast to civilian society in 1965.

At Fort Benning, where Powell was in the class ahead of his, Captain John Cash heard the buzz that the war was getting bigger. Eager to go to Vietnam, he went to the personnel officer, who called the Pentagon and granted Cash his wish. Like Powell and so many others, John Cash believed that there was no better place for a confident young black man than the military.

Cash spent most of his first Vietnam tour, in 1965–1966, as a captain in the 1st Battalion of the 7th Cavalry. The "First of the Seventh" was the best battalion in the brigade—with "quality leadership," Cash said.

The best kind of commander, Colonel Harold G. Moore, tall and taciturn, was a soldier's soldier who respected his troops regardless of their color. Cash said he would have given his life for

Moore, who taught him "what it was to be a soldier." Moore called his 1965 soldiers the Kennedy Class, meaning the class that heard Kennedy's famous charge in his Inaugural Address on January 20, 1961: "Ask not what your country can do for you—ask what you can do for your country." The Army that was great in race relations and morale was also great in idealism and courage.

Twenty-four-year-old Specialist 5 Calvin Bouknight from Washington, D.C., and twenty-three-year-old Second Lieutenant Dennis Deal, a white ROTC graduate of Duquesne University, were two more members of Moore's Kennedy Class. Twenty-six-year-old Captain George Forrest, commander of Alpha Company, 1st Battalion of the 5th Cavalry, was another gung-ho "Kennedy Class" officer. As a black officer, he told me, he was happy in the Army, because the Army judged him only by his ability to "do the job."

A ROTC graduate of Morgan State University, Forrest had chosen to enter the military for job security. Joining Benning's basic officer course in January 1961, he moved on to Fort Ord and, later, to Germany with the 1st Infantry Division. In 1963, he was chosen for the "Old Guard," the presidential Honor Guard in Washington, based at Fort Meyer. He served at President Kennedy's funeral.

Back at Benning, Forrest joined the test unit 11th Air Assault Division, the future 1st Cavalry (Airmobile). In August 1965, he went to Vietnam. There were no black brigade or battalion commanders in the 1st Cavalry, but Forrest was one of several black combat company commanders, four of whom were Morgan State graduates and fraternity brothers.

Idealism was not the only thing that George Forrest, Dennis Deal, Calvin Bouknight, Harold Moore, and John Cash shared in common. Among other things, there was the experience of the first large-scale confrontation of the war, which took place in the Central Highlands of South Vietnam in mid-November 1965: the Battle of Ia Drang.

The Battle of Ia Drang began at Landing Zone (LZ) X-Ray, which was about the size of a football field and surrounded by brush.

Once Moore's battalion had been inserted, troops explored the nearby hills and mountains, looking for enemy to kill. The trouble was, the North Vietnamese had their own plan, with thousands of troops waiting near the edges of LZ X-Ray and in the nearby hills. No sooner had Moore and some elements of his battalion landed than the NVA pounced.

Lieutenant Dennis Deal's platoon was trapped in a hailstorm of bullets. Anyone who stood up was shot at. There were roughly a dozen wounded all around when Deal felt a foot stepping on his back. "Calvin was getting up," Deal recalled when we spoke some thirty years later.

Calvin Bouknight, the 3rd Platoon medic who had refused to carry a weapon because he didn't believe in killing, was the only man on his feet. Using his body to shield a wounded man, Bouknight knelt on one knee to provide first aid. Deal thought that Bouknight knew he was going to die. "He knew the situation—he saw guys on their knees being shot down." Miraculously, the medic was able to patch up two or three men. Less than five minutes after he began to treat the wounded, Bouknight was shot in the center of his spine.

At considerable personal risk, two soldiers (both white) ran up and carried Bouknight back for evacuation. Deal could see that

Bouknight was in "utter agony," with tears streaming down his face. "You're gonna make it, Calvin," said Deal.

"Sarge, I didn't make it." These were Bouknight's first, and last, words to the medical platoon sergeant at the aid station.

John Cash, on duty as 3rd Brigade assistant operations officer at the Catecka tea plantation headquarters, heard the battle at Ia Drang unfold over field radios. For John Cash, the atmosphere was "terrible," like a "morgue." The casualty count noted on the blackboard kept getting higher. Cash heard Moore on the radio asking for reinforcements. He estimated that he was up against five hundred to six hundred North Vietnamese, with more on the way.

Moore's men fought alone the rest of the day, as volunteer helicopter crews came in regularly, under fire, to evacuate the dead and wounded. The next morning's attack killed forty-two Americans and wounded nearly twenty. U.S. B-52s dropped bombs and fighters delivered napalm into the hills above X-Ray, where NVA troops were gathering to attack. Two days after the battle started, it ebbed away, as the North Vietnamese seemed to pull back. As Moore and the other survivors prepared to return to base camp, replacements and reinforcements arrived. Among them was Captain George Forrest's Alpha Company.

Going into X-Ray under small-arms fire was something Forrest would never forget. "There must have been about a thousand rotting bodies out there, starting at about twenty feet, surrounding the giant circle of foxholes."

Shortly after their arrival, Forrest and the other fresh troops were ordered to walk from X-Ray to LZ Albany, a clearing about two miles away where they were supposed to be picked up by helicopters. Instead, they walked into the second and even bloodier phase of the Ia Drang battle, in which 155 Americans were killed and another 121 wounded in close, fierce combat. More Americans were killed on the march toward LZ Albany than in any other single confrontation in Vietnam.

At midmorning on November 18, Lieutenant Colonel Robert McDade, commander of the operation, ordered all units to proceed to LZ Albany in a single, foolhardy column with no flanking protection (like Colin Powell's ARVN in the A Shau) Forrest's unit was at the rear. "I had no idea what guys in front were doing," he told me. He was worried about his men. It was unbearably hot; they had been up for two nights in a row.

Compounding the first blunder, McDade, in a move Forrest called "most unusual" and others called "disastrous," suddenly called all company leaders forward to the head of the column to discuss the capture of two NVA "scouts." Having all the company leaders in one place was as bad as giving credence to so-called captured NVA scouts.

Forrest, more than five hundred yards in the rear, moved, with his two radiomen, forward through McDade's other units. He did not like what he saw. "I saw guys sitting around smoking, drinking water," he said, "not in a position to respond."

The small-arms fire began almost as soon as Forrest reached the command post. The "scouts" were actually an NVA advance guard—it was a classic ambush. When the first rounds came in, Forrest immediately raced back to his company.

In their book, *We Were Soldiers Once . . . And Young,* Moore and journalist Joseph Galloway recounted Forrest's famous run— "down that six-hundred-yard-long gauntlet of fire, miraculously unscathed." They noted that his speed, "and the forming of his men into a defensive perimeter, helped keep Alpha Company . . . from sharing the fate of Charlie, Delta, and Headquarters companies of the 2nd Battalion in the middle of the column." During the four days of fighting, 234 Americans were killed. Enemy dead were estimated at some two thousand. On that basis, Westmoreland declared the battle a "victory." A week after Ia Drang, Westmoreland asked for roughly 41,000 more U.S. troops.

A month before the Battle of Ia Drang, in October 1965, the Air Force fighter pilot Colonel Fred V. Cherry, who had served in the Korean War, was shot down over North Vietnam and captured. He was the forty-third American pilot captured in the North, and the first black. After he was shot down and captured, Cherry was taken to Hoa Lo Prison, the "Hanoi Hilton."

Cherry's cell in the Hanoi Hilton had "the biggest rats you ever saw in your life." Every morning, he was taken to the place Americans called Heartbreak, a torture chamber with built-in leg irons. When Cherry was moved to Cu Loc Prison outside Hanoi (known as the Zoo), he got a cellmate: Lieutenant Porter Halyburton, a white Navy pilot from Tennessee shot down five days before him.

In February 1966, Cherry underwent surgery on his shoulder, which had been wounded when he was captured. He was put into a torso cast to his hip and was given no medication and no treatment. The incisions quickly got infected. He fell in and out of consciousness, was totally immobile. He had to depend on his cellmate to feed and wash him.

In March, Cherry went to the hospital to have the cast taken off. His weight was down from 135 to 80 pounds. "When they took the cast off, a lot of skin came off with it," Cherry later told journalist Wallace Terry. "Then they washed me down with gasoline out of a beer bottle. . . . I passed out from the fumes."

Cherry had two more operations, the last of which he endured without anesthetic. When he returned to his cell, blood was running down to his feet. Halyburton put him in his bunk, and they both cried. Four days later, Halyburton was removed from the cell and they wept again. "I never hated to lose anybody so much in my entire life."

Cherry was then tortured daily, and he had yet another operation, after which he was kept in solitary for fifty-three weeks. The interrogators wanted tapes and written statements denouncing the war and the American government. "If they are going to kill me, they are going to have to kill me," Cherry thought. "I'm just not going to denounce my government or shame my people."

Throughout all his ordeals, Cherry contemplated suicide. "I would just pray to the Supreme Being each morning for the best mind to get through the interrogations, and then give thanks each night for makin' it through the day." Cherry was finally sent home following a prisoner-of-war exchange in 1973.

In the spring of 1967, Colin Powell became a student at Army Command and General Staff College at Fort Leavenworth: it was the track for future generals. At the end of thirty-eight weeks Powell would be expected to know "how to move a division of twelve to fifteen thousand men by train or road, how to feed it, supply it, and, above all, fight it." By then, more and more U.S. troops had poured into Vietnam. Casualties on both sides rose, with no end in sight. The enemy continued to set the tempo of the war, determining when and where to engage.

Back in 1966, Secretary of Defense McNamara had instituted "Project 100,000." He portrayed this project as part of LBJ's Great Society program, as the president called his domestic policies, which included civil rights acts. Great Society initiatives in LBJ's War on Poverty included Operation Head Start, Job Corps, and Medicaid and Medicare.

McNamara's program drafted 100,000 men a year who otherwise would have been rejected, mainly for low grades on mental aptitude tests. McNamara asserted that his motive was to help disadvantaged young men. In reality, it was about "bodies": about the need for more and more men to send to Vietnam, where warfare was taking a terrible toll on civilians.

Military operations uprooted millions of Vietnamese people. Besides creating a generation of refugees, American weapons were killing and wounding uncounted Vietnamese children and adults. With bombs and napalm falling indiscriminately, civilian casualties often outweighed the military's. On the home front, Vietnam was inspiring the largest outpouring of public anti-war feeling in American history.

U.S. troop levels neared the 500,000 mark in 1967, and the war appeared to be stalemated. Late in the year, there were highly publicized and very bloody pitched battles in the highlands and along the Laotian border; U.S. infantry units and Marines were engaged exactly where their enemy wanted to fight.

During 1967, 9,300 Americans were killed in Vietnam. Nevertheless, according to Westmoreland, the prognosis was excellent. In November, he proclaimed, "The enemy's hopes are bankrupt." The general told Congress and the press in emphatic terms that the U.S. military, on the threshold of 1968, was becoming more and more successful all the time.

"The morning of February 1, 1968, I came out of the bedroom, put on the coffeepot, and turned on the TV news," wrote Colin Powell, still at Leavenworth. "I was stunned. There on the screen were American GIs fighting on the grounds of the U.S. embassy and ARVN forces battling before the Presidential Palace in the heart of Saigon."

It was the Tet offensive: the Vietcong and the NVA had launched coordinated attacks against Saigon, Danang, Hué, Pleiku, Kontum, Can Tho, and provincial and district capitals the length and breadth of South Vietnam. The offensive had started during the Vietnamese holiday celebrating the lunar new year, called Tet. "In cold military terms," Powell wrote, "the Tet offensive was a massive defeat for the Vietcong and North Vietnam." Powell added:

> *Their troops were driven out of every town they had attacked, and with horrific losses, estimated at 45,000 of the 84,000 men committed. . . . It did not matter how many of the enemy we killed. The Viet Cong and North Vietnam had all the bodies needed to fling into this conflict and the will to do so. The North simply started sending in its regular army units to counter the losses.*

The Tet offensive shattered the credibility of LBJ and Westmoreland, and more bad news followed. The siege of the Khe Sanh Marine base, which had begun in January, grew very grim. There was talk of nuclear weapons. Indeed, even before the siege began, Westmoreland had ordered a study of the feasibility of using nuclear weapons in the area, but government officials ordered him to stop. Unfortunately, military overzealousness was not put in check in time in the village of My Lai in Quang Ngai province.

On March 16, 1968, a unit of the 11th Brigade of the Americal Division launched an attack on My Lai. The reported body count was 128 enemy dead, without capture of any weapons. Westmoreland's command awarded the unit a special commendation for the large "body count." The American public later found out what really happened at My Lai: a massacre of innocent civilians, including many children and elderly people. The 128-victim count was only partial; there had actually been 347 victims.

Meanwhile, support for LBJ's policies ebbed as the fighting became more and more savage. Coincidentally, the day of the My Lai Massacre, JFK's brother Robert F. Kennedy, a committed liberal reformer, announced his candidacy for the presidency. Many believed that he would heal America's racial wounds and end the war.

Anti-war demonstrations spread across the country. On March 31, 1968, LBJ stunned the world with his announcement that he would not seek reelection in November. He also announced a partial bombing halt and said he would seek peace talks. A few days later, on April 4, Martin Luther King, Jr., who had been speaking out against the war since 1965, was assassinated in Memphis, Tennessee. In April 1967, in a speech at Riverside Church in New York City, King had made it clear that he opposed the war not just because of the disparity in black and white draft statistics, but also because the war was bankrupting poverty programs. King said he feared for "the health of our land" and for the American soul—lest it become "totally poisoned" by the war.

Following King's murder, 125 American cities erupted into flaming violence. This was far from the only time that such happened in the 1960s. Frustrated black urban youths, imprisoned by poverty and fed up with police brutality, had taken their fury and frustration into the streets during several summers. The summer of 1965 saw the worst riot in decades, when thirty-four people were killed during several days of rioting in Watts, a black section of Los Angeles.

Two months after King's murder, on June 6, after winning the California Democratic primary, Robert Kennedy died from an assassin's bullet. In August, the Democratic National Convention in Chicago was turned into a bloody spectacle in which Chicago police violently assaulted anti-war demonstrators.

By the fall of 1968, almost no one wanted war anymore. The Republican Richard Nixon campaigned for president on a "secret" (and nonexistent) plan to end the war and on the "southern strategy," which involved exploiting white backlash against the civil rights movement.

In a campaign film, Nixon appealed to "forgotten Americans." "They provide most of the soldiers who died to keep us free," Nixon said, as a close-up photo of a young black soldier in Vietnam appeared on the screen. Nixon's adviser Leonard Garment shook his head at an early viewing. "We can't show a Negro just as RN's saying 'most of the soldiers who died to keep us free,'" said Garment. "That's been one of their big claims all along—that the draft is unfair to them—and this could be interpreted in a way that would make us appear to be taking their side." The black soldier was replaced with a white one.

* * *

In July 1968, Colin Powell left Fort Leavenworth to return to Vietnam as executive officer, 3rd Battalion, 1st Infantry, 11th Infantry Brigade, Americal Division, in Quang Ngai province. It had been five years since Powell had been in Vietnam. "Deterioration of discipline and morale was obvious," he wrote. Powell moved his cot every night, partly to thwart the Vietcong, partly to avoid "attacks on authority from within the battalion itself." Incidents of "fragging" (the killing of officers by fragmentation grenades) were on the rise.

Shortly after Powell arrived in Vietnam, Americal Division commander Major General Charles M. Gettys chose him to be his G-3 (deputy chief of staff for operations and planning), a job that usually went to a lieutenant colonel. "Overnight," Powell wrote, "I went from looking after eight hundred men to planning warfare for nearly eighteen thousand troops, artillery units, aviation battalions, and a fleet of 450 helicopters."

As Colin Powell ended his second tour of Vietnam in 1969, so did Air Force Captain Neil R. Brooks, a descendant of veteran of the American Revolution Barzillai Lew. When I tried to figure out his great-great relationship, he laughed and said, "Just say I'm the seventh generation." Like his eminent ancestor, he was Massachusetts born and raised. Like Colin Powell, he was Distinguished Graduate of his 1964 Officer's Training School class.

From 1964 to 1967, as lieutenant and captain, Brooks spent the war at Clark Air Force Base in the Philippines as assistant director of administrative services for the 13th Air Force—responsible for all administrative services in the Philippines, Thailand, and Taiwan, with support for bases in Vietnam. Brooks was part of what made the Air Force function. (He became U.S. Representative to the North Atlantic Treaty Organization

[NATO] and retired in 1986 with a fifth Air Force Meritorious Service Medal.)

By 1968, the Army had the same race problems as American society. Confederate flags proliferated and black soldiers began more and more to opt for the Black Power movement, which rejected both nonviolence and integration. The black draftees of 1966 and 1967, who landed in Vietnam in 1968, were a new breed of black soldier. "The war had used up the professionals who found in military service fuller and fairer employment . . . and who found in uniform a supreme test of their black manhood," wrote journalist Wallace Terry in his book, *Bloods.*

Replacing the careerists were black draftees, many just steps removed from marching in the Civil Rights Movement or rioting in the rebellions that swept the urban ghettos from Harlem to Watts. All were filled with a new sense of black pride and purpose. They spoke loudest against the discrimination they encountered on the battlefield in decorations, promotions and duty assignments. They chose not to overlook the racial insults, cross-burnings and Confederate flags of their white comrades. They called for unity among black brothers on the battlefield to protest these indignities and provide mutual support. And they called themselves "Bloods."

While many young Americans sought to avoid the draft, others, like Merill Dorsey, were eager to get into uniform and go to Vietnam.

When he was a little boy, Merrill Dorsey saw a Marine Corps

uniform in the window of a recruiting office in Catonsville, Maryland, and resolved that one day he would be a Marine. But when he was thirteen years old, his left foot was severely damaged and deformed in a car accident. Dorsey underwent seven operations; doctors told him that standing up was going to be difficult for the rest of his life, let alone running and jumping, which were out of the question. "But my mind kept on saying, 'You can deal with this,' " Dorsey said. In 1968, when he was eighteen, Dorsey went to sign up with the Marines, and he was accepted, having managed to keep his socks on during the physical examination.

Dorsey excelled in boot camp on Parris Island, South Carolina, and went on to a training assignment at Camp Lejeune, North Carolina. Dorsey's disillusionment began when he was assigned to the camp's communications school, whose graduates would be entrusted with calling in air strikes and artillery bombardments and whose errors could be disastrous. When his class sat down for its final exam, the instructor wrote all the answers on the blackboard. The course had to produce bodies to go to Vietnam, trained or not. Dorsey protested, and he was reassigned to more infantry training, with special attention to detecting booby traps.

In early 1969, Dorsey left for Vietnam, where he was assigned to an area not far from Danang that he called Booby Trap Heaven. He performed very well in combat, but his disillusionment deepened. "Vietnam was a big mistake for everybody who was there," he said. The more he came to know his fellow Marines, he said, the more he realized that "basically a lot of them had nowhere to go. Most people had been in trouble on the outside—black and white. This was not what I imagined this whole thing was about."

After nearly six months in Vietnam, Dorsey was wounded and a Marine officer saw his left foot while he was in a hospital. Despite Dorsey's superb performance as a Marine and his fervent desire to return to his unit, he was going home. One could not have a foot like Dorsey's and still be a Marine, the officer had said. Dorsey eventually became part of a team at the John F. Kennedy Institute, a facility affiliated with Johns Hopkins University, for the care of handicapped children. He stayed for fifteen years, doing everything from clerical work to counseling troubled youngsters.

By the summer of 1969, the first U.S. military units had been withdrawn from Vietnam. While the overall U.S. troop level had begun to decline, fresh draftees still arrived every day to replace GIs who had finished their tours in the remaining units. And casualties remained appalling.

While peace talks continued in Paris, Nixon pursued the "Vietnamization" of the war. "Vietnamization" meant reducing the number of U.S. ground troops, turning the brunt of the fighting over to the ARVN, and supporting it with air strikes. In August of 1969, he sent his national security adviser, Henry Kissinger, to Paris to begin secret discussions with the North Vietnamese. In September, Ho Chi Minh, leader of the Vietminh, died. Two massive anti-war demonstrations occurred in Washington that autumn.

On May 4, 1970, Ohio National Guard troops killed four students at an anti-war rally at Kent State University. Within a week, protests and boycotts closed down more than four hundred college campuses across the country. On May 15, two students were killed by police during an anti-war protest at predominantly black Jackson State College, in Mississippi. Thirty-seven university presidents, in a signed letter of protest, blamed Nixon's policies for alienating the nation's youth.

In October 1970, John Saar of *Life* magazine wrote about an Army "in evolution"—an Army "trying to adjust to the winding-down war in Vietnam." It was also an Army that was becoming more and more bitter about the war. "Old ideas of dress, behavior, discipline and rank no longer apply," Saar wrote. "Virtually no draftee wants to be fighting in Vietnam anyway, and in return for his reluctant participation he demands, and gets, personal freedoms."

GIs wore peace-symbol medallions. Black ones also sported symbols of black pride, such as the Afro. Stories about troops refusing direct orders appeared in the press, as did accounts of "fraggings." Marijuana had long been popular. In 1970 and 1971, "scag" (a very powerful heroin) flooded Vietnam and reached thousands of young soldiers.

In February 1971, South Vietnamese troops with U.S. air support invaded Laos. By April, the U.S. death toll in Vietnam was a little over 45,000. In June 1971, Daniel Ellsberg, a State Department official who had served in Vietnam in the mid-1960s, gave to *The New York Times* and other newspapers copies of the "Pentagon Papers," a top-secret Defense Department study of U.S. decision making in Vietnam. The Pentagon Papers made it clear that over the years policy makers had consistently and deliberately lied to Congress and the American people about Vietnam.

In January 1972, President Nixon announced that Henry Kissinger had for some time been carrying on secret negotiations with the North Vietnamese about ending the war. In February, Nixon and Kissinger visited Mao Tse-tung and Chou En-lai in

China, again raising hopes for peace. As U.S. troop levels and casualties declined, Vietnam receded from the headlines.

The war came back with startling ferocity at the end of March with the Easter Offensive, in which the North Vietnamese sent the ARVN reeling in panicky, headlong flight in several parts of the country. Nixon ordered the bombing of Hanoi and Haiphong and the mining of Haiphong harbor. Only massive tactical B-52 strikes kept the rampaging NVA at bay before the fighting ebbed away. In the midst of the offensive, Nixon operatives broke into the Watergate offices of the Democratic National Committee and were promptly caught. The incident attracted little attention at the time and was not a significant issue in the presidential campaign.

Democratic presidential candidate George McGovern ran on a pledge to get America out of Vietnam immediately. By October 1972, President Nixon had a plan that was acceptable to North Vietnam but not to South Vietnam. Nevertheless, Kissinger announced that "peace is at hand" shortly before election day. Nixon trounced McGovern, but the war did not end.

South Vietnam's President Nguyen Van Thieu continued to balk at signing the treaty. To reassure South Vietnam that the United States was still its ally, Nixon and Kissinger unleashed a mammoth, eleven-day B-52 assault on North Vietnam at Christmastime, killing many civilians, including some patients at the Bach Mai civilian hospital in Hanoi. North Vietnamese anti-aircraft fire shot down some of the bombers, and more U.S. pilots became prisoners of war.

On January 27, 1973, in Paris, the war in Vietnam came to its official end (as did the draft in the United States). Representatives of the United States, North Vietnam, South Vietnam, and the

Vietcong, otherwise known as the Provisional Revolutionary Government, signed a peace treaty, with several provisions. There was to be an immediate cease-fire and prisoner-of-war exchange, and all remaining U.S. troops had to leave Vietnam within sixty days. North Vietnam was not to reinforce its troops in South Vietnam or seek reunification by other than peaceful means. On March 29, 1973, the last planeload of U.S. troops lifted off from Tan Son Nhut airfield in Saigon.

Some fifty U.S. military attachés remained, and there was no doubt that the war would continue as it did in Cambodia, where heavy U.S. bombing against Communist forces (begun secretly in March 1969) went on until August 14, 1973, when Congress ordered it stopped. On the surface at least, the war entered a lull, during which the North sent men and supplies toward the South in great quantities on the Ho Chi Minh trail.

Thieu's regime clung to the hope that the United States would always rescue it with B-52 strikes, peace agreement or not, if the North Vietnamese decided to mount an offensive. But Richard Nixon's options in Vietnam narrowed as the Watergate scandal deepened and ultimately led to his resignation on August 9, 1974. Vice President Gerald Ford became the thirty-eighth president. He pardoned Nixon on September 8.

While Nixon was president, nearly 21,000 Americans were killed in Vietnam, and another 53,000 were seriously wounded. We will never know how many casualties occurred throughout Indochina during the war.

On March 11, 1975, North Vietnamese forces captured Ban Me Thuot, in the Central Highlands, and touched off a rout. ARVN units disintegrated. By March 25, northern troops had seized Hue. By March 30, they had Danang and were headed for

Saigon. In Cambodia, Communist forces, known as the Khmer Rouge, were closing in on the capital, Phnom Penh. The U.S. embassy staff pulled out on April 13 and the Khmer Rouge entered the city four days later. Thieu and other top Saigon officials fled on April 25 and the last American officials in Vietnam lifted off from the roof of the Saigon embassy by helicopter on April 29. The next day, North Vietnamese tanks clanked past the embassy and toward Thieu's palace. The war was over.

Career officers and soldiers who returned home were assimilated and welcomed on bases: the professional military protected its own. But many draftees, returning to civilian communities, found an indifferent welcome at best.

"When I got back to the real world, it seemed nobody cared that you'd been to Vietnam," one veteran complained to Wallace Terry. "As a matter of fact, everybody would be wondering where have you been for so long. They would say, how did you lose your leg? In a fight? A car wreck? Anything but Vietnam." Others felt so unwelcome and so alienated that they turned to the counterculture or to crime. Vietnam veterans of all races would find that they often had more in common with each other than with civilians of their own race. Both agreed that coming home was, in its own way, as hard as combat.

The war in Vietnam had come close to destroying the moral fabric of the military as well as the country. Hands down, this had been the worst American war. The future American military byword would be "No more Vietnams."

DESERT STORM

For an African-American, the military is the fairest place to reach goals based on potential. In the military, standards are very clear. If you are good and you've met the standards, you will be promoted.

—Lieutenant General Calvin Waller, deputy commander of Operation Desert Storm, in an interview with author

" The Iraqi army had made me uncomfortable ever since Iraq and Iran ended their bloody eight-year war in 1988," wrote Colin Powell in his autobiography, *My American Journey*. "Once Saddam, with an army over one million men strong, no longer had Iran to worry about, I feared he would look for mischief somewhere else." By 1988, Powell was a four-star general. He was also President Ronald Reagan's national security adviser. In August 1989, President George Herbert Walker Bush named him chairman of the Joint Chiefs of Staff, the Defense Department's highest military post. A little less than a year later, Powell's concern about Iraq's president, Saddam Hussein, making "mischief" deepened.

On July 17, 1990, Saddam Hussein publicly threatened Kuwait and the United Arab Emirates with war. Hussein accused these nations of putting a "poisoned dagger" into his nation's back by producing too much oil and thereby driving down the price of oil. Iraq had an enormous debt from its war with Iran. Hussein was hoping to raise oil prices.

By July 31, 100,000 Iraqi troops, including the elite Republican Guard with hundreds of new Soviet tanks, were amassed in southern Iraq, on the border with Kuwait. General Powell was concerned enough to call General H. Norman Schwarzkopf at MacDill Air Force Base, in Tampa. As commander in chief of Central Command, Schwarzkopf was responsible for military activities in southern Asia, the Horn of Africa, and the Middle East. A military conflict in which Iraq was the aggressor was his "worst case" Middle East scenario. "The world's fourth-largest army," wrote Schwarzkopf, "was sitting just north of oil fields whose output was essential to the industrialized world."

On August 2, Iraqi troops invaded Kuwait. Later that day, President George Bush told a pool of TV reporters that the United States was "not discussing intervention." On August 3, in Washington, D.C., Schwarzkopf explained to the president and the National Security Council just why Iraq figured in a worst-case scenario. In size, Saddam Hussein's standing army ranked behind only China's, the Soviet Union's, and Vietnam's. (The U.S. armed forces ranked seventh.) Iraq had 900,000 men in sixty-three divisions, including eight of the Republican Guard, and an arsenal of international weapons: Soviet tanks, South African heavy artillery, Chinese and Soviet rocket launchers, Chinese and French anti-ship missiles, Soviet bombers, and French Mirage fighters. The CIA estimated that Iraq had at least a thousand tons of chemical weapons.

Things took a turn for the worse on August 5, when the Iraqi Republican Guard began massing tanks and artillery on the Saudi Arabian border. At that point, President Bush declared that the invasion of Kuwait "will not stand" and committed America to the liberation of Kuwait and the defense of Saudi Arabia.

Schwarzkopf and Secretary of Defense Richard B. Cheney

flew to Saudi Arabia to brief that nation's King Fahd. As Schwarzkopf wrote in his book, *It Doesn't Take a Hero,* he wanted to be sure that "the king understood that we were talking about flooding his airfields, harbors, and military bases with tens of thousands more Americans than Saudi Arabia had ever seen." Soon, the first U.S. fighter planes landed. By the third week of August, the defensive operation in the Persian Gulf had a name: Operation Desert Shield.

President Bush had determined in early August that America's diplomatic efforts should be "massive" in order to mobilize world opinion against Iraq. The United Nations condemned the invasion that month and officially voted to use force to expel Iraqi forces from Kuwait in November. Personnel, matériel, or both would come from more than thirty nations. This coalition included Afghanistan, Argentina, Australia, Belgium, Britain, Canada, Czechoslovakia, Egypt, France, Italy, Kuwait, New Zealand, Niger, Norway, Oman, Pakistan, the Philippines, Poland, Saudi Arabia, Senegal, Sierra Leone, Singapore, South Korea, Spain, Syria, Turkey, and the United States. The latter would provide by far the most troops: 540,000.

What turned out to be the largest U.S. force fielded since Vietnam was unlike any military organization in American history. It was integrated and coed. By 1973, when the All Volunteer Force was born, Uncle Sam wanted *motivation,* not just bodies. The military wanted young people who were looking for job training, travel opportunities, and college funds. Like many other Americans, blacks saw military service as a great opportunity. Prior to Iraq's invasion of Kuwait, many in the military didn't imagine that they would ever see their nation engaged in a full-scale war.

*   *   *

U.S. troops began arriving in Saudi Arabia in early September. Powell visited them on October 21. He worried about the troops' patience. "Troops would fight for each other and for certain core values: national survival, the lives of American citizens," he wrote later. "They would fight for their leaders—presidents, even generals, if the reasoning was presented clearly and honestly." But it was "problematical," he believed, whether they would fight for long for another country, like Kuwait, or simply to punish a Saddam.

Ten days after Powell visited the troops, President Bush decided to double the number of U.S. forces in Saudi Arabia, sending three more aircraft carriers, a second Marine division, and the tank-heavy VII Corps from Germany. The target date for the ground war was sometime in mid-February 1991. In December 1990, on his second visit to Saudi Arabia, Powell told the troops to be ready for war.

Working with Powell and Schwarzkopf on war preparation and planning was Lieutenant General Calvin Waller. These three men had all been young officers in Vietnam and had worked together before. Waller and Schwarzkopf had been classmates at Fort Leavenworth. Powell and Waller had worked together daily at the Pentagon in the late 1970s and early 1980s, when both were senior military assistants at the Department of Defense. Schwarzkopf had been Waller's commanding officer at General Staff College. They had served together again in the early 1980s, when Schwarzkopf (with three stars) was commander, and Waller (with two stars) was his chief of staff.

While Powell, Schwarzkopf, and Waller were preparing for war, the United Nations had given Iraq a new deadline for withdrawal from Kuwait: January 15. On January 12, the U.S. Congress officially authorized the use of force against Iraq. Three days later, Saddam Hussein ignored the U.N. deadline.

As coalition forces were being readied for action, there was concern and debate about whether such a war would spark trouble in the Middle East. "If the United States goes to war against Iraq, it could cause a heck of a backlash in the Arab world," the U.S. ambassador to Saudi Arabia, Charles Freeman, had told Schwarzkopf in early October. "I'm not sure anyone in Washington has given that enough thought." Schwarzkopf realized that two conditions were necessary to placate the Arab world. "First, Arab forces in significant numbers had to fight by our side; second, we had to win." In the event of a ground war against Iraq, he determined that Arab forces must be the ones to liberate Kuwait City.

When the air campaign against Iraq began on January 17, Schwarzkopf suggested that the name of the operation, having shifted to an offensive one, be changed to Operation Desert Storm.

In the first days of the war, Schwarzkopf copied out a quote from the memoirs of Civil War general William T. Sherman: "War is the remedy our enemies have chosen. And I say let us give them all they want."

On the first day of Desert Storm, Powell thought of a saying of Civil War general Robert E. Lee: "It is well that war is so terrible, or we should grow too fond of it." Powell realized how much he loved preparing for war and he had to remind himself that this was real, and that many Americans would die in Desert Storm.

By the end of the first day, U.S. bombs had destroyed every known Scud missile site in western Iraq, and only two U.S. planes had been downed. The Scud missile was, in Powell's words, "a cheap, crude, inaccurate Soviet engine of destruction" that had proved an effective terror weapon against civilians in the Iran-Iraq War.

On the second day, Powell and Cheney briefed the press. "I explained the battle plan," Powell wrote. "We were using our air-power first to destroy the Iraqis' air defense system and their command, control, and communications to render the enemy deaf, dumb, and blind. We then intended to tear apart the logistics supporting their army in Kuwait, including Iraqi military installations, factories, and storage depots." Powell was proud of his punch line: "Our strategy in going after this army is very simple. First we are going to cut it off, and then we are going to kill it."

The second day also saw Scud missile attacks on Israel, and on January 19, two U.S. fighter pilots were shot down during a hastily planned mission to attack missile-storage bunkers in western Iraq. Ten days later, an Iraqi armored division attacked along the Saudi-Kuwaiti border, overwhelming the Saudi army at Al Khafji—which U.S. forces helped Saudi Arabia regain.

Despite initial heavy Scud attacks on Riyadh, the capital of Saudi Arabia, by the last week in January, wrote Schwarzkopf, "the skies over Iraq belonged to the coalition." And "we were accomplishing exactly what we had set out to do: cripple Iraq's military system while leaving its agriculture and commerce intact and its civilian population largely unharmed."

On the night of January 21, a twenty-seven-year-old black first lieutenant, Phoebe Jeter, of Sharon, South Carolina, the only woman to direct the launch of a Patriot missile during the war, shot down a Scud aimed at Riyadh. She told her story to *People* magazine.

There had been "no time to think" when she saw the "TBM" (tactical ballistic missile) on her "green scope" coming directly at them. "All around I could hear the BOOM! BOOM! BOOM! of other Patriot units beginning to fire. The van began to rock." There were so many Scuds, Jeter said, that her scope "looked like popcorn." The attack, which looked to people outside the van like something from *Star Wars*, lasted less than five minutes but seemed much longer. Jeter said that she used to be "scared of the dark" before she joined the Army. "When we all started congratulating each other later on about how well we did, about the four Scuds the Patriots took down that night, I felt so proud," she said. "I thought to myself, 'I can do anything. Anything I put my mind to, I can do.'"

"Braver." After the war, that's what Major Flossie Satcher said being in the Army had made her. As a high school senior, Satcher had heard her friends and classmates talking about the Reserves and how "exciting" it was. Enlisting in the Mississippi National Guard, Satcher won a ROTC scholarship to Jackson State University and went into the Army right after graduation. She was looking for "travel" and "adventure." Like most reservists of her generation, never in her life did she expect to go to war. A single mother of twin daughters, Satcher was a twenty-five-year-old first lieutenant in October 1990 when she went to Saudi Arabia as part of the 24th Ordnance Company. Their job was to provide ammunition for the 24th Infantry Division of the XVIII Airborne Corps.

Thirty-five thousand American women had served in World War I, ten thousand of them overseas. Nearly 400,000 served in

World War II, where military nurses in the Pacific became prisoners of war. About 7,500, mostly nurses, served in Vietnam. Some 30,000 women served in Desert Storm, about 6 percent of the 540,000 U.S. forces. Two women became prisoners of war; twenty-one were wounded in action; and fifteen, of ranks from private to major, died, five of them in hostile action. They were pilots, truck drivers, MPs, and water-purification experts. By federal law, women could not serve in direct combat, but they were increasingly serving in combat support groups perilously near the front. Thanks to the performance of women in Desert Storm, in 1991 Congress enacted measures to permit women to become combat pilots in the Air Force, Navy, Army, and Marines.

Few large National Guard units served in Vietnam. In contrast, 53,000 members of the National Guard went to the Persian Gulf. Many would find themselves too close to combat for comfort.

New York's 719th Transportation Company, formerly the 369th Infantry Regiment, World War I's Harlem's Own, was the first National Guard unit from New York to reach Saudi Arabia. Captain Dennis Bush, a New York City police officer, was commander of this mostly black and Hispanic company.

Most of the unit were civil servants, including New York City transit employees, sanitation workers, teachers, and firefighters and police officers. Many were Vietnam veterans. Their average age was forty, although the range was twenty-two to fifty-five. The 719th went to Saudi Arabia in early November 1990, in support of the 101st Air Assault Division. The 719th's major duty was driving semi-trailers and keeping the front lines supplied with everything from computers to armored personnel carriers. They named their base Guardian City, after both the National Guard and the Guardians, a black police fraternal organization.

The company included one female officer and twelve enlisted women. One of these women was Sergeant Alvie Grimes, an accountant. Grimes had joined the National Guard in 1983 for extra pay. A November 1990 article published in *The New York Times*, "From Harlem to Saudi Arabia," quotes Grimes as saying, "It's a good cause." She also said, "I never expected to be here. I've been enjoying the benefits for seven years, and now it's time to do what I was trained to do."

The air phase of Desert Storm lasted thirty-eight days. The ground war, launched in mid-February, lasted all of four.

On February 8, Cheney and Powell went to Riyadh for a final review of ground-war plans, and Schwarzkopf told them that he was ready. "Where once had been nothing but desert, a pipeline, and an occasional Bedouin tent," he wrote, "there now were seas of camouflage . . . that I knew concealed thousands of tons of food, spare parts, fuel, water, and munitions for the offensive."

Saudi Arabian troops and U.S. Marines were poised on the eastern end of the Saudi-Kuwaiti border, Egyptians spearheaded the pan-Arab corps on the western end, and the U.S. VII Corps was arriving from Germany to tactical assembly areas near the front. The U.S. Navy had its big guns ready in the Persian Gulf, and British troops and French Legionnaires were in position on the Saudi border.

The assembled force was enormous, and strategic air strikes had already accomplished their vital mission. But as the air campaign moved from striking government buildings and infrastructure to bombing Iraqi forces, the Republican Guard and their tanks simply went underground into bunkers. On February 13, the targeted strike on the Al Firdos air raid bunker in a suburb of Baghdad, the capital of Iraq, killed more than two hundred civilians. The incident led to immediate restrictions on strategic bombing. Meanwhile, a broadcasting and leafleting campaign was urging Iraqi troops to defect, advising them to "March towards Mecca," the direction of the U.S. front lines.

The opening of the ground war was set for February 24. Yet again, Saddam Hussein was given a deadline for withdrawal: noon on February 23. Yet again, he ignored it. On the day of the deadline, U.S. Army Special Forces troops were inserted deep inside Iraq, and Stealth fighters attacked Iraqi intelligence headquarters (unaware that American POWs were inside—none of whom were killed).

At four A.M. Saudi time on February 24, the first Marines, led by M-60 tanks and Cobra helicopters and followed by thousands of troops in armored carriers and humvees, crossed the Saudi-Kuwaiti border in darkness and cold rain, under covering fire from 155mm howitzers. At six A.M. Saudi time, President Bush appeared on television to declare that "the liberation of Kuwait has now entered a final phase."

The Kuwaiti resistance reported that the Iraqis were destroying Kuwait City, with explosions throughout the city. But help was on the way: two Saudi armored brigades and a combined pan-Arab brigade, the victors of Al Khafji. Some three hundred miles to the west, a French light armored division and a brigade from the 82nd Airborne were on their way to Al Salman air base, home of the Scuds that fell on Riyadh. Thirty miles east of Al Salman, the biggest helicopter assault in history, slightly delayed by rain and fog, was about to begin.

"More than three hundred Apache, Cobra, Blackhawk, Huey, and Chinook helicopters, piloted by men and women, were transporting an entire brigade with its humvees, howitzers, and tons of fuel and ammunition fifty miles into Iraq," wrote Schwarzkopf. "They were to set up a huge firebase from which attack helicopters could easily strike the Euphrates valley."

The main attack force, with sixteen hundred heavy tanks, was waiting on the Saudi border. It had three objectives: to free Kuwait City, the job of the pan-Arab corps; to destroy the Republican Guard, the job of VII Corps; and to close Iraqi escape routes in the Euphrates valley, the job of the 24th Infantry Division.

By midmorning, coalition troops had reported little real opposition and taken many prisoners of war. "After firing a few shots," wrote Schwarzkopf, "the Iraqis just climbed out of trenches and gave themselves up." By the second day of the ground war, the Marines had so many prisoners, and so few trucks available to transport them, that they were simply taking their weapons and pointing south, directing them to "Walk that way."

Bad news came on the second day: VII Corps, whose job was to take out the Republican Guard, was behind schedule. The long-term success of Operation Desert Storm depended upon the success of VII Corps. Worse news came from Al Khobar in Saudi Arabia: the U.S. Army barracks had been destroyed by a Scud attack. Twenty-eight U.S. soldiers were dead; ninety-eight were wounded. Twenty-year-old Private Adrienne Mitchell, a black member of a noncombat Army Supply Unit, was one of three women killed in the attack. "I did 30 years [and] didn't get a scratch," Mitchell's father, a retired Air Force master sergeant, told *Newsweek.* "My daughter's been in for five months, and she's dead."

By noon Saudi time on February 26, VII Corps was finally in the thick of the fight, having almost destroyed one Republican Guard division, the Tawakalna, and driven two others, the Medina and Hammurabi, into retreat toward Basra, Iraq. The enemy was being driven directly into what the Air Force called the kill box— the four-lane highway leading from Kuwait City to Basra. The bombing was intense. Between air strikes Americans flew overhead, telling Iraqis in Arabic, "Get out of your vehicles, leave them behind, and you will not die."

Meanwhile, U.S. Marines and the pan-Arab forces were linking up to liberate Kuwait City. VII Corps fought off the elusive Medina Division all night, and Kuwaiti, Saudi, Egyptian, and other Arab troops officially liberated Kuwait City on the morning of February 27. That afternoon Powell told Schwarzkopf to think about "wrapping up" the war. The United States already had, in Powell's words, a "prisoner catch" of up to seventy thousand. "The doves are starting to complain about all the damage you're doing," Schwarzkopf reported Powell as saying. For public relations purposes, the Bush Administration wanted the war to last an even one hundred hours.

The debate over how far to advance into Iraq was already in full cry. All along Bush had been characterizing Saddam Hussein as the devil incarnate. This did not help Americans to understand why he was allowed to stay in power, but the danger of destabilizing the Arab world was brought up in every debate. Meanwhile, the last Iraqi escape route, the highway from Kuwait City to

Basra, had become what Powell called "a shooting gallery" for U.S. planes. The Highway of Death is what the media called it. "The road was choked with fleeing soldiers and littered with the charred hulks of nearly fifteen hundred military and civilian vehicles," Powell remembered. Inside many of those vehicles were the bodies of Iraqi soldiers who had ignored or failed to hear the coalition message to flee.

To supply ammunition close up, Major Flossie Satcher's unit had followed the 24th Infantry Division into Iraq on the Highway of Death. At the tail end of the line, Satcher's unit saw burning vehicles and bodies on fire. The desert wind was so strong that she knew that she was inhaling floating particles of burning bodies.

In a matter of days, U.S. and coalition forces had liberated Kuwait; 75 percent of the Iraqi army had deserted or surrendered; the Republican Guard had been routed; Iraq was basically bombed back to the Stone Age; and Kuwait was on the brink of ecological disaster because of burning oil wells. One hundred forty-seven Americans had died in combat. Two hundred thirty-six had died in accidents and of other causes, including "friendly fire." A tentative U.S. estimate of Iraqi losses would be 100,000 killed and 300,000 wounded.

There would always be critics of the decision not to totally destroy the Republican Guard and deal Saddam Hussein and his regime a death blow. Overall, however, Operation Desert Storm was considered a success. Although led by Vietnam veterans, Desert Storm had been everything Vietnam was not. It had been swift, victorious, with relatively few U.S. casualties and high troop morale. It had also been, by and large, popular with Americans.

The victory parade in June in New York City was a blizzard of ticker tape, confetti, and balloons. "The celebrations were no doubt out of proportion to the achievement," Powell wrote. "We had not fought another World War II. Yet, after the stalemate of Korea and the long agony in [Vietnam], the country was hungry for victory. . . . American people fell in love again with their armed forces. The way I look at it, if we got too much adulation for this one, it made up for the neglect the troops had experienced coming home from those other wars."

No war in U.S. history had seen more blacks in leadership positions—from General Colin Powell and Lieutenant General Calvin Waller to three members of the Patriot missile crew decorated for shooting down Scud missiles over Riyadh. Blacks, about 12 percent of the U.S. population, had made up 20 percent of the total U.S. troops: some 30 percent of the Army, 22 percent of the Navy, 17 percent of the frontline Marines, and 13 percent of the Air Force. Of the American soldiers killed, 15 percent were black. Eighteen-year-old Army private Robert D. Talley, a black man from Newark, New Jersey, killed in a "friendly fire" incident, was the youngest soldier to die. The oldest was a fifty-eight-year-old black veteran of the Korean War, First Sergeant Joseph Murphy, of New York's 102nd Maintenance National Guard Unit.

At the start of the war, John Roberts, a white fourth-grade teacher in a predominantly black and Hispanic school in Oklahoma City, asked his class to "adopt" Navy Petty Officer Harold Mansfield, Jr. Mansfield's mother had been a teacher in the same school. Mrs. Mansfield's husband had died eleven months before her son went to the Persian Gulf. Roberts wanted to "cheer her up."

The children wrote letters to Harold Mansfield. They kept his picture on the bulletin board and drew pictures of the ship on which he served, the U.S.S. *Saratoga*. When Mansfield came home in April, the class gave him a party, with popping balloons and a cake with a design of the *Saratoga*. There were hugs and speeches, and many of the boys said that they wanted to be like Mansfield when they grew up. He impressed the children even further by demonstrating his job in Desert Storm: writing flight information backward so people on the flight deck could read it. On clear laminated plastic, Mansfield wrote "Everyone can be a hero" backward.

Three weeks later, the children learned that in a grocery store parking lot in Florida, a member of the white supremacist organization Church of the Creator had shot Mansfield dead. Their teacher wrote "white supremacist" on the blackboard and told the children to look up "supremacist" in the dictionary.

The children's first reactions were violent: they wanted to "fry" Mansfield's killer in the electric chair or drown him. Seeking a positive outlet for their rage, their teacher suggested that the children write to him instead.

"Why did you kill our hero?" they asked again and again. About twenty children went to the funeral, each carrying a rose for Mansfield's mother.

EPILOGUE

In the wake of Desert Storm, because of Powell's success and publicity, more Americans were becoming aware of past and present black military heroes. And the military was ready not only to celebrate its black heroes but also to apologize for past injustices. Because the history was long and the injustices rife, belated rewards for a job well done came only to a representative handful. The few, most of them long dead, would have to stand in for the many. These brave people were honored throughout the 1990s in ceremonies that evoked tears, pride, and some anger as the government and the military made their mea culpas.

These apologies included a memorial, dedicated in Concord, California, in July 1994, to the 320 sailors, mostly black ammunition loaders, who were killed in the July 1944 explosion at Port Chicago, California. Five years later, eighty-year-old Freddie Meeks, one of two surviving members of the fifty sailors convicted of mutiny after the explosion, was pardoned by President Clinton. Meeks, who served only seventeen months of his fifteen-year sentence thanks to Thurgood Marshall's defense, was proven not to have mutinied but, in fact, to have volunteered for other duty. "I knew God was keeping me around for something," he said in an interview, which ran in a December 1999 issue of *The New York Times*. "But I am just sorry so many of the others are not around to see it."

In 1995, the Air Force announced that the official reprimands against 101 Tuskegee Airmen who had staged a sit-in at the illegally segregated officers' club at Freeman Field, Indiana, in 1945, would be expunged from their records. In 1997, Walterboro,

South Carolina, which had shown greater hospitality in World War II to German and Italian prisoners of war than to black American pilots, honored the Tuskegee Airmen with a monument. In 1998, eighty-five-year-old General Benjamin O. Davis, Jr., of the Tuskegee Airmen, received his fourth star after years of lobbying by the men who'd flown under him.

The Medal of Honor, the nation's highest award for valor, bestowed only by the president, was symbolically the most important mea culpa of them all. It was at last bestowed upon Corporal Freddie Stowers of World War I's 371st Regiment. The Army admitted it had made a "mistake." Stowers's commanding officer had recommended him for the Medal of Honor in September 1918 for actions on the infamous Hill 188 during the Champagne Offensive. In May 1991, President Bush presented the Medal of Honor to Freddie Stowers's eighty-eight-year-old sister. Staff Sergeant Douglas Warren of the 101st Airborne Division, Stowers's great-great-nephew, was flown in from Saudi Arabia to be part of the White House ceremony.

On January 13, 1997, President Clinton awarded Medals of Honor to seven black men for their extraordinary valor in World War II. "History has been made whole today," Clinton said, "and our nation is bestowing honor on those who have long deserved it." Accepting the medals were brothers, sisters, widows, and children. Only one veteran among the seven was alive to receive his own gold medal, with its sky-blue ribbon and glass and wood presentation case. That man was Lieutenant Vernon Baker of the 370th Regiment, 92nd Division.

Baker was cited for actions in Italy in 1945 at Castello Aghinolfi. There, leading an advance on a German-held castle, he single-handedly killed eight Germans and destroyed an enemy observation post and an enemy dugout. Then, with about two-thirds of the twenty-five men with him killed or injured by enemy machine-gun and mortar fire, Baker volunteered to cover the withdrawal of the walking wounded and, in the process, destroyed two enemy machine-gun stations.

"I was a soldier and I had a job to do," Baker was quoted as saying in a 1997 article in *The New York Times*. But he admitted that risking his life for his country while serving in a segregated unit was "kind of rough." Still, he never lost hope in the possibility of change. "I knew things would get better, and I'm glad to say that I'm here to see it," Baker said. "The only thing that I can say to those that are not here with me is, thank you, fellas, well done. And I will always remember you."

They were patriots, each and every one of them, along with hundreds of thousands of other black Americans who served in their nation's military from the Revolution through Desert Storm and beyond.

SELECTED BIBLIOGRAPHY

Allen, Robert L. *The Port Chicago Mutiny*. New York: Warner Books, 1989.

Anderson, Trezzvant W. *Come Out Fighting: The Epic Tale of the 761st Tank Battalion*. Long Island, NY: 761st Tank Battalion and Allied Veterans Association, 1979.

Blair, Clay. *The Forgotten War: America in Korea, 1950–1953*. New York: Times Books, 1987.

Bowers, William T., William M. Hammond, and George L. MacGarrigle. *Black Soldier, White Army: The 24th Infantry in Korea*. Washington, D.C.: United States Army Center of Military History, 1996.

Burchard, Peter. *One Gallant Rush: Robert Gould Shaw and His Brave Black Regiment*. New York: St. Martin's Press, 1965.

Bussey, Charles M. *Firefight at Yechon: Courage and Racism in the Korean War*. Washington, D.C.: Brassey's, 1991.

Cash, John. *Seven Firefights in Vietnam*. Washington, D.C.: Office of the Chief of Military History, United States Army, 1970.

Cashin, Herschel V. *Under Fire with the Tenth U.S. Cavalry*. New York: Bellwether Publishing, 1970.

Collum, Danny Duncan, ed. *African Americans in the Spanish Civil War*. New York: G. K. Hall, 1992.

Cornish, Dudley Taylor. *The Sable Arm: Black Troops in the Union Army, 1861–1865*. Lawrence, KS: University Press of Kansas, 1987.

Dalfiume, Richard M. *Desegregation of the U.S. Armed Forces*. Columbia, MO: University of Missouri Press, 1969.

Davis, Benjamin O., Jr. *Benjamin O. Davis, Jr.: American.* Washington, D.C.: Smithsonian Institution Press, 1991.

Downey, Bill. *Uncle Sam Must Be Losing the War.* San Francisco: Strawberry Hill Press, 1982.

Drotning, Phillip T. *Black Heroes in Our Nation's History: A Tribute to Those Who Helped Shape America.* New York: NTC/Contemporary Publishing, 1969.

Earley, Charity Adams. *One Woman's Army.* College Station, TX: Texas A & M University Press, 1989.

Emilio, Luis F. *A Brave Black Regiment: The History of the Fifty-Fourth Regiment of Massachusetts Volunteer Infantry, 1863–1865.* Salem, NH: Ayer Co., 1990.

Farwell, Byron. *Over There: The United States in the Great War, 1917–1918.* New York: W. W. Norton, 1999.

Fish, Hamilton. *Memoir of an American Patriot.* Washington, D.C.: Regnery Publishing, 1991.

Fleming, Thomas. *Liberty!* New York: Viking Press, 1997.

Fletcher, Marvin E. *America's First Black General: Benjamin O. Davis, Sr., 1880–1970.* Lawrence, KS: University Press of Kansas, 1989.

———. *The Black Soldier and Officer in the United States Army, 1891–1917.* Columbia, MO: University of Missouri Press, 1974.

Flipper, Henry Ossian. *The Colored Cadet at West Point.* Salem, NH: Ayer Co., 1986.

Foner, Jack D. *Blacks and the Military in American History.* New York: Praeger, 1974.

Francis, Charles E. *The Tuskegee Airmen.* Boston: Branden Publishing Company, 1988.

Gordon, Michael R., and General Bernard E. Trainor. *The Generals' War.* Boston: Little Brown & Co., 1995.

Haywood, Harry. *Black Bolshevik.* Chicago: Lake View Press, 1978.

Heywood, Chester D. *Negro Combat Troops in the World War.* Worcester, MA: Commonwealth Press, 1928.

Johnson, Jesse J. *Roots of Two Black Marine Sergeants Major.* Hampton, VA: Carver Publishing, 1978.

Kaplan, Sidney, and Emma Nogrady Kaplan. *The Black Presence in the Era of the American Revolution.* Amherst, MA: University of Massachusetts Press, 1989.

Karnow, Stanley. *Vietnam: A History.* New York: Penguin Books, 1984.

Keegan, John. *The First World War.* New York: Knopf, 1999.

Langguth, A. J. *Patriots: The Men Who Started the American Revolution.* New York: Simon & Schuster, 1988.

Lawson, Don. *The Abraham Lincoln Brigade.* New York: Ty Crowell Co., 1989.

Little, Arthur W. *From Harlem to the Rhine.* New York: Covici-Friede Publishers, 1936.

MacGregor, Morris J., Jr. *Integration of the Armed Forces 1940–1965.* Washington, D.C.: Center of Military History, United States Army, 1981.

McPherson, James M. *Battle Cry of Freedom: The Civil War Era.* New York: Ballantine Books, 1988.

Moore, Lieutenant General Harold G., Ret., and Joseph L. Galloway. *We Were Soldiers Once . . . and Young.* New York: Harper Perennial, 1993.

Moskos, Charles C., and John Sibley Butler. *All That We Can Be: Black Leadership and Racial Integration the Army Way.* New York: Basic Books, 1996.

Motley, Mary Penick. *The Invisible Soldier.* Detroit: Wayne State University Press, 1987.

Muller, William G. *The Twenty Fourth Infantry Past and Present.* Fort Collins, CO: The Old Army Press, 1972.

Nalty, Bernard C. *Strength for the Fight: A History of Black Americans in the Military.* New York: Free Press, 1986.

Nankivell, John H. *Buffalo Soldier Regiment: History of the 25th Infantry 1869–1926.* Fort Collins, CO: The Old Army Press, 1972.

Nell, William C. *The Colored Patriots of the American Revolution.* Salem, NH: Ayer Co., 1986.

Phelps, J. Alfred. *Chappie: America's First Black Four-Star General.* Novato, CA: Presidio Press, 1991.

Powell, Colin, with Joseph E. Persico. *My American Journey.* New York: Random House, 1995.

Quarles, Benjamin. *The Negro in the American Revolution.* New York: W. W. Norton, 1973.

Rose, Robert A. *Lonely Eagles.* Los Angeles: Tuskegee Airmen, 1976.

Schlesinger, Arthur M., Jr. *The Bitter Heritage: Vietnam and American Democracy 1941–1966.* Boston: Houghton Mifflin, 1966.

Schwarzkopf, General H. Norman. *It Doesn't Take a Hero.* New York: Bantam Books, 1993.

Shaw, Henry I., Jr., and Ralph W. Donnelly. *Blacks in the Marine Corps.* Washington, D.C.: History and Museums Division Headquarters, U.S. Marine Corps, 1975.

Terry, Wallace. *Bloods: An Oral History of the Vietnam War by Black Veterans.* New York: Ballantine Books, 1984.

Thomas, Hugh. *The Spanish Civil War.* New York: Harper & Row, 1961.

Ward, Geoffrey C., with Ric Burns and Ken Burns. *The Civil War: An Illustrated History.* New York: Knopf, 1990.

Yates, James. *Mississippi to Madrid.* Seattle, WA: Open Hand Publishing, 1989.

SUGGESTED READING

Clinton, Catherine. *The Black Soldier: 1492 to the Present*. Boston: Houghton Mifflin, 2000.

Cooper, Michael L. *Hell Fighters: African American Soldiers in World War I*. New York: Lodestar, 1997.

Cox, Clinton. *The Forgotten Heroes: The Story of the Buffalo Soldiers*. New York: Scholastic, 1993.

————. *Undying Glory: The Story of the Massachusetts 54th Regiment*. New York: Scholastic, 1991.

Hansen, Joyce. *Between Two Fires: Black Soldiers in the Civil War*. New York: Franklin Watts, 1993.

Haskins, Jim. *Black, Blue & Gray: African Americans in the Civil War*. New York: Simon & Schuster, 1998.

————. *Black Eagles: African Americans in Aviation*. New York: Scholastic, 1995.

McKissack, Patricia and Frederick. *Red-Tail Angels: The Story of the Tuskegee Airmen of World War II*. New York: Walker & Co., 2001.

Mettger, Zak. *Till Victory Is Won: Black Soldiers in the Civil War*. New York: Lodestar, 1994.

Pfeifer, Kathryn Browne. *The 761st Tank Battalion*. Brookfield, CT: Twenty-First Century Books, 1994.

Stovall, Taressa. *The Buffalo Soldiers*. New York: Chelsea House, 1997.

INDEX